LEARN TYPESCRIPT

100+ Coding Q&A

Yasin Cakal

Code of Code

CONTENTS

INTRODUCTION

Welcome to "Learn Typescript," the ultimate book for learning the popular programming language. Typescript is a supercharged version of JavaScript that provides optional static typing, class-based object-oriented programming, and other advanced features. In this book, you will learn everything you need to know to get started with Typescript and start using it in your projects.

Throughout this book, you will learn the fundamentals of Typescript, including its syntax, types, variables, interfaces, classes, functions, and more. You will also learn how to use advanced Typescript features like enums, decorators, namespaces, and modules.

This book is designed for both beginners and experienced programmers who want to learn Typescript and take their skills to the next level. Whether you are a web developer, mobile developer, or just looking to expand your programming skills, this book has something for you.

So if you're ready to learn the power of Typescript and start using it in your projects, join us in "Learn Typescript" today and take your programming skills to the next level!

WHAT IS TYPESCRIPT AND WHY SHOULD YOU LEARN IT?

Typescript is a popular programming language that was developed and maintained by Microsoft. It is a supercharged version of JavaScript that provides optional static typing, class-based object-oriented programming, and other advanced features. In this article, we will explore what Typescript is, why it was created, and why you should consider learning it.

What is Typescript?

Typescript is a programming language that is a superset of JavaScript, meaning that any valid JavaScript code is also valid Typescript code. However, Typescript adds additional features to JavaScript that make it more powerful and easier to use. These features include:

- Static typing: In Typescript, you can specify the type of a variable or function parameter, which can help catch errors at compile time rather than runtime. This can make your code more predictable and easier to debug.
- Class-based object-oriented programming: Typescript supports class-based object-oriented programming, which means you can create classes, define properties and methods, and use inheritance. This can make your code more organized and reusable.
- Advanced features: Typescript also includes other advanced features like interfaces, enums, decorators, and type aliases, which can make your code more expressive and easier to read.

Why was Typescript Created?

Typescript was created by Microsoft in 2012 to address some of the challenges of developing large-scale applications in JavaScript. At the time, JavaScript was increasingly being used to build complex client-side applications, but it did not have some of the features that developers were used to in other languages like static typing and class-based object-oriented programming.

Microsoft saw the opportunity to create a language that could provide these features while still being compatible with the vast ecosystem of JavaScript libraries and frameworks. They also wanted to create a language that would be easy for JavaScript developers to learn and adopt.

As a result, they created Typescript, which has since become one of the most popular programming languages in the world.

Why Should You Learn Typescript?

Now that you know what Typescript is and why it was created, you may be wondering why you should consider learning it. Here are a few reasons why Typescript might be a good choice for you:

- Improved productivity: The static typing and advanced features in Typescript can help you write code faster and with fewer errors. This can lead to increased productivity and fewer debugging headaches.
- Better code quality: Typescript's static typing and other features can help ensure that your code is more predictable and easier to maintain. This can lead to better code quality and a more stable application.
- Improved teamwork: Typescript's static typing and other features make it easier for different team members to work together on the same codebase. This can improve collaboration and make it easier to integrate changes from different team members.
- Widely used: Typescript is used by many large companies and is supported by popular libraries and frameworks like Angular and React. This means that learning Typescript can open up more job opportunities and make it easier for you to work on a variety of projects.
- Easier learning curve: If you already know JavaScript, learning Typescript will likely be easier for you since it is a superset of JavaScript. This means that you can leverage your existing knowledge of JavaScript and quickly start using Typescript in your projects.

Conclusion

In conclusion, Typescript is a powerful programming language that was created to address some of the challenges of developing large-scale applications in JavaScript. It provides advanced features like static typing and class-based object-oriented programming, which can improve productivity, code quality, teamwork, and more. It is also widely used and has a relatively easy learning curve for those already familiar with JavaScript.

If you are a programmer looking to take your skills to the next level, learning Typescript could be a great investment of your time and effort. It is a versatile language that is used in a variety of projects and can open up more job opportunities in the industry. So if you're ready to learn the power of Typescript, start your journey today and see what it can do for you and your projects.

Exercises

To review these concepts, we will go through a series of exercises designed to test your understanding and apply what you have learned.

What is Typescript and how does it relate to JavaScript?
What are some benefits of using static typing in Typescript?
What are some advanced features of Typescript?
Why was Typescript created?
Why should you consider learning Typescript?

Solutions

What is Typescript and how does it relate to JavaScript?
Typescript is a programming language that is a superset of JavaScript, meaning that any valid JavaScript code is also valid Typescript code. However, Typescript adds additional features to JavaScript that make it more powerful and easier to use, such as static typing and class-based object-oriented programming.

What are some benefits of using static typing in Typescript?

Some benefits of using static typing in Typescript include: improved productivity, better code quality, improved teamwork, and a wider range of job opportunities. Static typing can help catch errors at compile time rather than runtime, which can make your code more predictable and easier to debug. It can also make it easier for different team members to work together on the same codebase and improve collaboration.

What are some advanced features of Typescript?

Some advanced features of Typescript include interfaces, enums, decorators, and type aliases. These features can make your code more expressive and easier to read, and can help you write code faster and with fewer errors.

Why was Typescript created?

Typescript was created by Microsoft in 2012 to address some of the challenges of developing large-scale applications in JavaScript. At the time, JavaScript was increasingly being used to build complex client-side applications, but it did not have some of the features that developers were used to in other languages like static typing and class-based object-oriented programming. Microsoft saw the opportunity to create a language that could provide these features while still being compatible with the vast ecosystem of JavaScript libraries and frameworks.

Why should you consider learning Typescript?

There are several reasons why you should consider learning Typescript, including improved productivity, better code quality, improved teamwork, and wider use in the industry. Typescript's static typing and other features can help ensure that your code is more predictable and easier to maintain, which can lead to better code quality and a more stable application. It is also widely used and supported by popular libraries and frameworks like Angular and React, which can open up more job opportunities and make it easier for you to work on a variety of projects. Additionally, if you already know JavaScript, learning Typescript may be easier for you since it is a superset of JavaScript.

SETTING UP A TYPESCRIPT DEVELOPMENT ENVIRONMENT

In this article, we will walk through the process of setting up a development environment for Typescript, including how to install the necessary tools and configure your project. Whether you are new to Typescript or just need a refresher on setting up a development environment, this article will provide all the information you need to get started.

Prerequisites

Before you can set up a Typescript development environment, you will need to have a few things installed on your machine:

- Node.js: Typescript is built on top of Node.js, so you will need to have it installed on your machine in order to use Typescript. You can download and install the latest version of Node.js from the official website (https://nodejs.org).
- A text editor or integrated development environment (IDE): You will also need a text editor or IDE to write and edit your Typescript code. Some popular options include Visual Studio Code, Sublime Text, and WebStorm. Choose the one that you are most comfortable with or that best fits your workflow.

Install Typescript

Once you have Node.js and a text editor or IDE installed, you are ready to install Typescript. There are a few different ways to do this, but the most common method is to use the Node Package Manager (npm).

To install Typescript using npm, open a terminal or command prompt and type the following command:

```
npm install -g typescript
```

This will install the latest version of Typescript globally on your machine, which means you will be able to use it from any directory.

You can also install Typescript as a dev dependency for a specific project by running the following command in the root directory of your project:

```
npm install --save-dev typescript
```

This will install Typescript locally for your project and add it to your package.json file.

Create a Typescript Configuration File

Once you have Typescript installed, you will need to create a configuration file to specify how your project should be compiled. To create a configuration file, open a terminal or command prompt and navigate to the root directory of your project. Then, type the following command:

```
tsc --init
```

This will create a file called "tsconfig.json" in the root directory of your project. The tsconfig.json file contains a set of options that control how your project is compiled.

Some of the options you can specify in the tsconfig.json file include:

- "target": This option specifies the version of JavaScript that your project should be compiled to. The default value is "es5," but you can also specify "es6," "es2015," or other versions.
- "outDir": This option specifies the directory where the compiled JavaScript files should be placed. By default, the compiled files are placed in the same directory as the source files.
- "rootDir": This option specifies the root directory for your source files. By default, it is set to the current directory.
- "strict": This option enables strict type checking in your project. When strict type checking is enabled, the compiler will enforce stricter type checking rules and report more errors.

For a full list of options that you can specify in the tsconfig.json file, you can consult the official documentation (https://www.typescriptlang.org/docs/handbook/tsconfig-json.html).

Compile Typescript to JavaScript

Now that you have Typescript installed and a tsconfig.json file set up, you are ready to compile your Typescript code to JavaScript. To do this, open a terminal or command prompt and navigate to the root directory of your project. Then, type the following command:

```
tsc
```

This will compile all of the Typescript files in your project according to the options specified in your tsconfig.json file. The compiled JavaScript files will be placed in the directory specified by the "outDir" option.

If you want to compile a specific file or files, you can specify them as arguments to the tsc command, like this:

```
tsc file1.ts file2.ts
```

You can also use the "–watch" option to tell the compiler to watch for changes to your Typescript files and automatically recompile them when they change. For example:

```
tsc --watch
```

This can be useful for development when you want to see your changes reflected in the compiled

JavaScript files in real-time.

Integrate Typescript with Your Text Editor or IDE

To get the most out of Typescript, you will want to integrate it with your text editor or IDE. Most text editors and IDEs have plugins or extensions that add Typescript support, including syntax highlighting, code completion, and error checking.

For example, if you are using Visual Studio Code, you can install the Typescript extension by following these steps:

1. Open the Extensions tab in Visual Studio Code.
2. Search for "Typescript" in the extensions marketplace.
3. Click "Install" to install the Typescript extension.
4. Restart Visual Studio Code to activate the extension.

Once the Typescript extension is installed, you will have access to all of the features it provides, including syntax highlighting, code completion, and error checking.

Conclusion

In conclusion, setting up a Typescript development environment is a straightforward process that involves installing the necessary tools, creating a configuration file, and integrating with your text editor or IDE. By following the steps outlined in this article, you will be able to start writing and compiling Typescript code in no time.

With a solid development environment in place, you can start exploring the features of Typescript and seeing how it can improve your projects. So get started today and see what Typescript can do for you!

Exercises

To review these concepts, we will go through a series of exercises designed to test your understanding and apply what you have learned.

What are the prerequisites for setting up a Typescript development environment?
How do you install Typescript using npm?
How do you create a Typescript configuration file?
How do you compile Typescript to JavaScript?
How do you integrate Typescript with your text editor or IDE?

Solutions

What are the prerequisites for setting up a Typescript development environment?
The prerequisites for setting up a Typescript development environment are: having Node.js installed on your machine, and having a text editor or IDE. Node.js is necessary because Typescript is built on top of it, and a text editor or IDE is needed to write and edit your Typescript code.

How do you install Typescript using npm?

To install Typescript using npm, open a terminal or command prompt and type the following command:

```
npm install -g typescript
```

This will install the latest version of Typescript globally on your machine, which means you will be able to use it from any directory.

How do you create a Typescript configuration file?
To create a Typescript configuration file, open a terminal or command prompt and navigate to the root directory of your project. Then, type the following command:

```
tsc --init
```

This will create a file called "tsconfig.json" in the root directory of your project. The tsconfig.json file contains a set of options that control how your project is compiled.

How do you compile Typescript to JavaScript?
To compile Typescript to JavaScript, open a terminal or command prompt and navigate to the root directory of your project. Then, type the following command:

```
tsc
```

This will compile all of the Typescript files in your project according to the options specified in your tsconfig.json file. The compiled JavaScript files will be placed in the directory specified by the "outDir" option.

How do you integrate Typescript with your text editor or IDE?
To integrate Typescript with your text editor or IDE, you will need to install a plugin or extension that adds Typescript support. Most text editors and IDEs have such a plugin or extension available, and you can usually find and install it through the built-in extensions marketplace.

For example, if you are using Visual Studio Code, you can install the Typescript extension by following these steps:

1. Open the Extensions tab in Visual Studio Code.
2. Search for "Typescript" in the extensions marketplace.
3. Click "Install" to install the Typescript extension.
4. Restart Visual Studio Code to activate the extension.

Once the Typescript extension is installed, you will have access to all of the features it provides, including syntax highlighting, code completion, and error checking.

BASIC TYPESCRIPT SYNTAX AND TYPES

Welcome to the "Basic Typescript Syntax and Types" section of our course "Learn Typescript"! In this article, we will cover the fundamentals of Typescript syntax and types, including variables, functions, and basic data types. By the end of this article, you should have a good understanding of these concepts and be able to start writing simple Typescript programs.

Variables

In Typescript, you can declare variables using the "let" or "const" keywords. The "let" keyword is used to declare variables that can be reassigned later, while the "const" keyword is used to declare variables that cannot be reassigned.

For example, the following code declares two variables using the "let" keyword:

```
let x = 10;
let y = 20;
```

You can also specify the type of a variable when declaring it by using a type annotation. For example:

```
let x: number = 10;
let y: string = 'hello';
```

In this example, the type of "x" is "number" and the type of "y" is "string". Typescript will check that you are assigning values of the correct type to these variables, and it will give you an error if you try to assign a value of the wrong type.

Functions

In Typescript, you can define functions using the "function" keyword followed by the function name, a list of parameters in parentheses, and a block of code in curly braces. For example:

```
function add(x: number, y: number): number {
  return x + y;
}
```

In this example, the function "add" takes two parameters of type "number" and returns a value of type "number". You can specify the return type of a function using a type annotation after the list of parameters, as shown in the example.

You can also define functions using the "arrow function" syntax, which is a shorter and more concise way of defining functions. For example:

```
const add = (x: number, y: number): number => x + y;
```

In this example, the function "add" is defined using the arrow function syntax and has the same behavior as the previous example.

Basic Data Types

Typescript supports a variety of basic data types, including numbers, strings, booleans, and null and undefined.

Numbers: Typescript has two types for representing numbers: "number" and "bigint". The "number" type represents a double-precision floating-point number, which is a number with a decimal point. The "bigint" type represents a large integer value. You can specify a number literal as a "number" by adding a decimal point or an exponent, or you can specify it as a "bigint" by adding the "n" suffix. For example:

```
let x: number = 10;
```

```
let y: bigint = 10n;
```

In this example, the variable "x" is of type "number" and the variable "y" is of type "bigint".

Strings: Typescript has a single type for representing strings, called "string". You can specify a string literal by enclosing it in single or double quotes. For example:

```
let x: string = 'hello';
```

```
let y: string = "world";
```

Booleans: Typescript has a single type for representing boolean values, called "boolean". You can specify a boolean literal by using the "true" or "false" keywords. For example:

```
let x: boolean = true;
```

```
let y: boolean = false;
```

Null and Undefined: Typescript has two types for representing the absence of a value: "null" and "undefined". The "null" type represents the intentional absence of a value, while the "undefined" type represents the default value for variables that have not been assigned a value. You can specify a null or undefined literal by using the "null" or "undefined" keywords. For example:

```
let x: null = null;
```

```
let y: undefined = undefined;
```

In this example, the variable "x" is of type "null" and the variable "y" is of type "undefined".

Union Types

In addition to the basic data types described above, Typescript also supports union types, which allow you to specify that a variable can be of multiple types. You can specify a union type by separating the individual types with a pipe (|) symbol.

For example, the following code defines a variable "x" that can be either a "string" or a "number":

```
let x: string | number;
```

You can then assign values of either type to the variable "x":

```
x = 'hello';
```

```
x = 10;
```

Type Aliases

Typescript also supports type aliases, which allow you to create a new name for an existing type. You can define a type alias using the "type" keyword followed by the alias name and the existing type. For example:

```
type ID = string | number;
```

In this example, the type alias "ID" is defined as a union of "string" and "number". You can then use the "ID" type in the same way you would use a basic data type:

```
let x: ID;
```

```
x = '123';
```

```
x = 456;
```

Type aliases can be especially useful when you need to use a complex type multiple times in your code, or when you want to give a more descriptive name to a type.

TypeScript has a number of other advanced features, including interfaces, classes, and enums, which we will cover in future sections of our course.

Conclusion

In conclusion, this article has covered the basics of Typescript syntax and types, including variables, functions, basic data types, union types, and type aliases. With this knowledge, you should now be able to start writing simple Typescript programs and using Typescript to type-check your code. In the next sections of our course, we will dive deeper into the advanced features of Typescript and explore how to use them to build larger and more complex applications.

Exercises

To review these concepts, we will go through a series of exercises designed to test your understanding and apply what you have learned.

What is the difference between the "let" and "const" keywords in Typescript?
How do you specify the type of a variable in Typescript?
How do you define a function in Typescript?
What are the basic data types in Typescript?
What are union types in Typescript?

Solutions

What is the difference between the "let" and "const" keywords in Typescript?

The "let" keyword is used to declare variables that can be reassigned later, while the "const" keyword is used to declare variables that cannot be reassigned. For example:

```
let x = 10;
x = 20; // valid
const y = 10;
y = 20; // invalid
```

In this example, the variable "x" is declared using the "let" keyword and can be reassigned, while the variable "y" is declared using the "const" keyword and cannot be reassigned.

How do you specify the type of a variable in Typescript?

To specify the type of a variable in Typescript, you can use a type annotation after the variable name. For example:

```
let x: number = 10;
let y: string = 'hello';
```

In this example, the type of "x" is "number" and the type of "y" is "string". Typescript will check that you are assigning values of the correct type to these variables, and it will give you an error if you try to assign a value of the wrong type.

How do you define a function in Typescript?

To define a function in Typescript, you can use the "function" keyword followed by the function name, a list of parameters in parentheses, and a block of code in curly braces. For example:

```
function add(x: number, y: number): number {
  return x + y;
}
```

In this example, the function "add" takes two parameters of type "number" and returns a value of type "number". You can specify the return type of a function using a type annotation after the list of parameters, as shown in the example.

You can also define functions using the "arrow function" syntax, which is a shorter and more concise way of defining functions. For example:

```
const add = (x: number, y: number): number => x + y;
```

What are the basic data types in Typescript?

The basic data types in Typescript are: "number", "string", "boolean", "null", and "undefined".

The "number" type represents a double-precision floating-point number, which is a number with a decimal point. The "bigint" type represents a large integer value. You can specify a number literal as a "number" by adding a decimal point or an exponent, or you can specify it as a "bigint" by adding the "n" suffix.

The "string" type represents a sequence of characters. You can specify a string literal by enclosing it in single or double quotes.

The "boolean" type represents a boolean value, which can be either "true" or "false".

The "null" type represents the intentional absence of a value.

The "undefined" type represents the default value for variables that have not been assigned a value.

What are union types in Typescript?

Union types in Typescript allow you to specify that a variable can be of multiple types. You can specify a union type by separating the individual types with a pipe (|) symbol. For example:

```
let x: string | number;
```

In this example, the variable "x" is defined as a union of "string" and "number", which means it can be assigned values of either type.

You can use union types to allow for more flexibility in your code, or to represent values that can take on multiple different types. For example, a function that returns a string or a number might be defined as follows:

```
function getResult(): string | number {
 // logic to determine the result goes here
 return 'success'; // or return 42;
}
```

In this example, the function "getResult" is defined as returning either a "string" or a "number", depending on the result of the logic inside the function.

UNDERSTANDING THE DIFFERENT TYPES IN TYPESCRIPT (E.G. NUMBER, STRING, BOOLEAN)

Welcome to the "Understanding the Different Types in TypeScript" section of our course "Learn TypeScript"! In this article, we will cover the various types available in TypeScript, including numbers, strings, and booleans. By the end of this article, you should have a good understanding of these types and be able to use them effectively in your TypeScript programs.

Numbers

TypeScript has two types for representing numbers: "number" and "bigint". The "number" type represents a double-precision floating-point number, which is a number with a decimal point. The "bigint" type represents a large integer value. You can specify a number literal as a "number" by adding a decimal point or an exponent, or you can specify it as a "bigint" by adding the "n" suffix. For example:

```
let x: number = 10;
let y: bigint = 10n;
```

In this example, the variable "x" is of type "number" and the variable "y" is of type "bigint".

TypeScript also supports the standard arithmetic operators for numbers, such as "+", "-", "*", and "/". For example:

```
let x: number = 10;
let y: number = 20;
let z: number = x + y; // 30
```

In this example, the variables "x" and "y" are both of type "number" and the result of their addition is also of type "number".

Strings

TypeScript has a single type for representing strings, called "string". You can specify a string literal by enclosing it in single or double quotes. For example:

```
let x: string = 'hello';
let y: string = "world";
```

In this example, the variables "x" and "y" are both of type "string".

TypeScript also supports the standard string operations, such as concatenation, interpolation, and slicing. For example:

```
let x: string = 'hello';
let y: string = 'world';
let z: string = x + ' ' + y; // 'hello world'
let a: number = 10;
let b: string = `the value of a is ${a}`; // 'the value of a is 10'
let c: string = 'hello world';
let d: string = c.slice(0, 5); // 'hello'
```

In this example, the variables "z" and "b" are both of type "string" and are created using concatenation and interpolation, respectively. The variable "d" is also of type "string" and is created by slicing the string "c".

Booleans

TypeScript has a single type for representing boolean values, called "boolean". You can specify a boolean literal by using the "true" or "false" keywords. For example:

```
let x: boolean = true;
let y: boolean = false;
```

In this example, the variable "x" is of type "boolean" and has a value of "true", while the variable "y" is also of type "boolean" and has a value of "false".

TypeScript also supports the standard boolean operations, such as "and" (&&), "or" (||), and "not" (!). For example:

```
let x: boolean = true;
let y: boolean = false;
let a: boolean = x && y; // false
let b: boolean = x || y; // true
let c: boolean = !x; // false
```

In this example, the variables "a", "b", and "c" are all of type "boolean" and are created using the "and", "or", and "not" operations, respectively.

Other Types

In addition to numbers, strings, and booleans, TypeScript also has several other types that you may encounter in your code. These include:

- "null" and "undefined": These types represent the absence of a value. The "null" type represents the intentional absence of a value, while the "undefined" type represents the default value for variables that have not been assigned a value. You can specify a null or undefined literal by using the "null" or "undefined" keywords.

- "void": This type represents the absence of a return value for a function. You can specify a void type by using the "void" keyword.
- "never": This type represents a value that will never occur. You can specify a never type by using the "never" keyword.

Conclusion

In conclusion, this article has covered the basic types in TypeScript, including numbers, strings, and booleans. You should now have a good understanding of these types and how to use them in your TypeScript programs. In future sections of our course, we will cover more advanced types, such as union types and type aliases, and how to use them to build larger and more complex applications.

Exercises

To review these concepts, we will go through a series of exercises designed to test your understanding and apply what you have learned.

What are the two types for representing numbers in TypeScript?
How do you specify a string literal in TypeScript?
What are the standard string operations in TypeScript?
How do you specify a boolean literal in TypeScript?
What are the other types in TypeScript besides numbers, strings, and booleans?

Solutions

What are the two types for representing numbers in TypeScript?
The two types for representing numbers in TypeScript are "number" and "bigint". The "number" type represents a double-precision floating-point number, while the "bigint" type represents a large integer value. You can specify a number literal as a "number" by adding a decimal point or an exponent, or you can specify it as a "bigint" by adding the "n" suffix.

How do you specify a string literal in TypeScript?
To specify a string literal in TypeScript, you can enclose it in single or double quotes. For example:

```
let x: string = 'hello';
let y: string = "world";
```

What are the standard string operations in TypeScript?
The standard string operations in TypeScript include concatenation, interpolation, and slicing. Concatenation allows you to combine multiple strings into a single string using the "+" operator. Interpolation allows you to insert the value of a variable into a string using the " ` " and "${}" syntax. Slicing allows you to extract a portion of a string using the "slice" method.

How do you specify a boolean literal in TypeScript?
To specify a boolean literal in TypeScript, you can use the "true" or "false" keywords. For example:

```
let x: boolean = true;
let y: boolean = false;
```

What are the other types in TypeScript besides numbers, strings, and booleans?

The other types in TypeScript besides numbers, strings, and booleans include "null", "undefined", "void", and "never". The "null" and "undefined" types represent the absence of a value, with "null" representing the intentional absence of a value and "undefined" representing the default value for variables that have not been assigned a value. The "void" type represents the absence of a return value for a function. The "never" type represents a value that will never occur.

DECLARING AND INITIALIZING VARIABLES IN TYPESCRIPT

Welcome to the "Declaring and Initializing Variables in TypeScript" section of our course "Learn TypeScript"! In this article, we will cover the various ways you can declare and initialize variables in TypeScript, including using the "let" and "const" keywords, destructuring, and the spread operator. By the end of this article, you should have a good understanding of these concepts and be able to use them effectively in your TypeScript programs.

Declaring Variables with "let" and "const"

TypeScript has two keywords for declaring variables: "let" and "const". The "let" keyword is used to declare variables that can be reassigned later, while the "const" keyword is used to declare variables that cannot be reassigned. For example:

```typescript
let x: number = 10;
x = 20; // valid
const y: number = 10;
y = 20; // invalid
```

In this example, the variable "x" is declared using the "let" keyword and can be reassigned, while the variable "y" is declared using the "const" keyword and cannot be reassigned.

It is generally a good idea to use "const" for variables that you do not need to change, as it helps to prevent accidental reassignments and makes your code easier to understand. However, there may be cases where you need to use "let", such as when you are using a loop variable or when you need to reassign a variable based on some condition.

Destructuring

TypeScript supports destructuring, which allows you to extract values from arrays and objects and assign them to separate variables. For example:

```typescript
let arr: number[] = [1, 2, 3];
let [a, b, c] = arr;
console.log(a); // 1
console.log(b); // 2
console.log(c); // 3
let obj: {x: number, y: number} = {x: 1, y: 2};
```

```
let {x, y} = obj;
console.log(x); // 1
console.log(y); // 2
```

In this example, we are using destructuring to extract values from an array and an object and assign them to separate variables. The variables "a", "b", and "c" are assigned the values from the array "arr", while the variables "x" and "y" are assigned the values from the object "obj".

Destructuring is a convenient way to extract values from arrays and objects, especially when you need to extract multiple values at once. It is also useful for creating variables with more descriptive names, as shown in the example above where we used "x" and "y" to represent the x and y coordinates of an object.

Spread Operator

TypeScript also supports the spread operator (…), which allows you to expand an array or object into separate values. For example:

```
let arr: number[] = [1, 2, 3];
let arr2: number[] = [...arr, 4, 5];
console.log(arr2); // [1, 2, 3, 4, 5]
let obj: {x: number, y: number} = {x: 1, y: 2};
let obj2: {x: number, y: number} = {...obj, z: 3};
console.log(obj2); // {x: 1, y: 2, z: 3}
```

In this example, we are using the spread operator to expand the array "arr" and the object "obj" into separate values. The array "arr2" is created by adding the values from "arr" and the additional values 4 and 5, while the object "obj2" is created by adding the values from "obj" and the additional value "z".

The spread operator is useful for creating new arrays and objects based on existing ones, or for combining multiple arrays or objects into a single one. It is also useful for creating shallow copies of arrays and objects, as the spread operator creates a new array or object rather than modifying the original one.

Conclusion

In conclusion, this article has covered the various ways you can declare and initialize variables in TypeScript, including using the "let" and "const" keywords, destructuring, and the spread operator. You should now have a good understanding of these concepts and be able to use them effectively in your TypeScript programs. In future sections of our course, we will cover more advanced topics, such as type inference and the "var" keyword, and how to use them to write more concise and maintainable TypeScript code.

Exercises

To review these concepts, we will go through a series of exercises designed to test your understanding and apply what you have learned.

What is the difference between the "let" and "const" keywords in TypeScript?

How do you extract values from an array or object using destructuring in TypeScript?

How do you expand an array or object into separate values using the spread operator in TypeScript?

How can you create a shallow copy of an array or object using the spread operator in TypeScript?

What are some benefits of using destructuring and the spread operator in TypeScript?

Solutions

What is the difference between the "let" and "const" keywords in TypeScript?

The "let" keyword is used to declare variables that can be reassigned later, while the "const" keyword is used to declare variables that cannot be reassigned. It is generally a good idea to use "const" for variables that you do not need to change, as it helps to prevent accidental reassignments and makes your code easier to understand. However, there may be cases where you need to use "let", such as when you are using a loop variable or when you need to reassign a variable based on some condition.

How do you extract values from an array or object using destructuring in TypeScript?

To extract values from an array or object using destructuring in TypeScript, you can use the following syntax:

```typescript
let arr: number[] = [1, 2, 3];
let [a, b, c] = arr;
let obj: {x: number, y: number} = {x: 1, y: 2};
let {x, y} = obj;
```

In this example, we are using destructuring to extract values from an array and an object and assign them to separate variables. The variables "a", "b", and "c" are assigned the values from the array "arr", while the variables "x" and "y" are assigned the values from the object "obj".

How do you expand an array or object into separate values using the spread operator in TypeScript?

To expand an array or object into separate values using the spread operator in TypeScript, you can use the following syntax:

```typescript
let arr: number[] = [1, 2, 3];
let arr2: number[] = [...arr, 4, 5];
let obj: {x: number, y: number} = {x: 1, y: 2};
let obj2: {x: number, y: number} = {...obj, z: 3};
```

How can you create a shallow copy of an array or object using the spread operator in TypeScript?

To create a shallow copy of an array or object using the spread operator in TypeScript, you can use the following syntax:

```typescript
let arr: number[] = [1, 2, 3];
let arr2: number[] = [...arr];
```

```
let obj: {x: number, y: number} = {x: 1, y: 2};
let obj2: {x: number, y: number} = {...obj};
```

In this example, we are using the spread operator to expand the array "arr" and the object "obj" into separate values, which are then assigned to the new variables "arr2" and "obj2". The spread operator creates a new array or object rather than modifying the original one, so "arr2" and "obj2" are shallow copies of "arr" and "obj".

What are some benefits of using destructuring and the spread operator in TypeScript?

There are several benefits to using destructuring and the spread operator in TypeScript:

- Destructuring allows you to extract values from arrays and objects and assign them to separate variables, which can be more convenient and easier to read than accessing the values directly.
- The spread operator allows you to expand an array or object into separate values, which is useful for creating new arrays and objects based on existing ones or for combining multiple arrays or objects into a single one.
- Both destructuring and the spread operator can help you write more concise and maintainable TypeScript code, as they allow you to write less boilerplate code and focus more on the logic of your program.

TYPE INFERENCE AND TYPE ANNOTATIONS

Welcome to the "Type Inference and Type Annotations" section of our course "Learn TypeScript"! In this article, we will cover the concept of type inference in TypeScript and how you can use type annotations to explicitly specify the types of your variables and functions. By the end of this article, you should have a good understanding of these concepts and be able to use them effectively in your TypeScript programs.

Type Inference

TypeScript has a feature called type inference, which allows the compiler to automatically infer the types of your variables and functions based on their values. For example:

```
let x = 10; // x is inferred to be of type number
let y = "hello"; // y is inferred to be of type string
function add(a: number, b: number): number {
  return a + b;
}
let result = add(1, 2); // result is inferred to be of type number
```

In this example, we are declaring three variables and a function, and the types of each of these are inferred by the TypeScript compiler based on the values they are assigned. The variable "x" is inferred to be of type number because it is assigned the value 10, which is a number. The variable "y" is inferred to be of type string because it is assigned the value "hello", which is a string. The function "add" is inferred to be of type function that takes two arguments of type number and returns a value of type number, based on the types specified in the function's signature. The variable "result" is inferred to be of type number because it is assigned the result of calling the "add" function, which is also of type number.

Type inference is a convenient feature in TypeScript, as it allows you to write code more quickly and with fewer errors. However, there may be cases where you need to explicitly specify the types of your variables and functions, in which case you can use type annotations.

Type Annotations

Type annotations allow you to explicitly specify the types of your variables and functions in TypeScript. They are used in the same way as type inference, but they provide more information to the compiler about the intended types of your code. For example:

```
let x: number = 10; // x is explicitly annotated as being of type number
let y: string = "hello"; // y is explicitly annotated as being of type string
function add(a: number, b: number): number {
  return a + b;
}
let result: number = add(1, 2); // result is explicitly annotated as being of type number
```

In this example, we are using type annotations to explicitly specify the types of our variables and functions. The variable "x" is annotated as being of type number, the variable "y" is annotated as being of type string, and the function "add" is annotated as being a function that takes two arguments of type number and returns a value of type number. The variable "result" is annotated as being of type number because it is assigned the result of calling the "add" function, which is also of type number.

Type annotations are useful in a few different situations:

- When you want to specify the types of your variables and functions more explicitly, to make your code easier to understand and maintain.
- When the TypeScript compiler is unable to infer the types of your variables and functions correctly, due to complex or unusual types.
- When you want to ensure that your code is typed.

TypeScript also has a special type called "any", which you can use to denote that a variable or function can have any type. This is useful when you do not know the type of a value or when you want to disable type checking for a specific part of your code. For example:

```
let x: any = 10; // x can have any type
x = "hello"; // x can now be a string
function add(a: any, b: any): any {
  return a + b;
}
let result = add(1, 2); // result can have any type
```

In this example, we are using the "any" type to disable type checking for the variables "x" and "result" and the function "add". This allows us to assign and return any type of value without generating a type error. However, it is generally a good idea to use "any" sparingly, as it can lead to less predictable and less maintainable code.

Conclusion

In conclusion, this article has covered the concepts of type inference and type annotations in TypeScript, and how you can use them to specify the types of your variables and functions. You should now have a good understanding of these concepts and be able to use them effectively in your TypeScript programs. In future sections of our course, we will cover more advanced topics, such as interfaces and classes, and how to use them to write more structured and reusable TypeScript code.

Exercises

To review these concepts, we will go through a series of exercises designed to test your understanding and apply what you have learned.

What is type inference in TypeScript, and how does it work?
What are type annotations in TypeScript, and when should you use them?
How do you use the "any" type in TypeScript?
How does TypeScript handle type compatibility for variables and functions?
How do type inference and type annotations work together in TypeScript?

Solutions

What is type inference in TypeScript, and how does it work?

Type inference in TypeScript is a feature that allows the compiler to automatically infer the types of your variables and functions based on their values. It works by examining the values that are assigned to your variables and the signatures of your functions, and inferring the most appropriate types based on these values. For example, if you assign a number value to a variable, the compiler will infer that the variable is of type number. If you define a function that takes two arguments of type number and returns a value of type number, the compiler will infer that the function is of type function that takes two arguments of type number and returns a value of type number.

What are type annotations in TypeScript, and when should you use them?

Type annotations in TypeScript are used to explicitly specify the types of your variables and functions. They provide more information to the compiler about the intended types of your code, and can be used in situations where the compiler is unable to infer the correct types, or when you want to specify the types more explicitly for clarity or maintenance purposes. You should use type annotations when you need to specify the types of your variables and functions more explicitly, or when the compiler is unable to infer the correct types due to complex or unusual types.

How do you use the "any" type in TypeScript?

The "any" type in TypeScript can be used to denote that a variable or function can have any type. To use the "any" type, you can specify it as the type annotation for your variable or function. For example:

```typescript
let x: any = 10; // x can have any type
function add(a: any, b: any): any {
  return a + b;
}
```

In this example, we are using the "any" type to disable type checking for the variables "x" and "result" and the function "add". This allows us to assign and return any type of value without generating a type error. However, it is generally a good idea to use "any" sparingly, as it can lead to less predictable and less maintainable code.

How does TypeScript handle type compatibility for variables and functions?

TypeScript checks the compatibility of variables and functions based on their types. A variable or function is considered compatible with another variable or function if it can be assigned or passed to it without generating a type error. For example, a variable of type number is compatible with a variable of type number or any, but not with a variable of type string. A function that takes two arguments of type number and returns a value of type number is compatible with a function that takes two arguments of type number and returns a value of type number or any, but not with a function that takes two arguments of type string and returns a value of type number.

How do type inference and type annotations work together in TypeScript?

Type inference and type annotations work together in TypeScript to help you specify the types of your variables and functions more accurately and efficiently. Type inference allows the compiler to automatically infer the types of your variables and functions based on their values, which can save you time and reduce the risk of type errors. Type annotations allow you to explicitly specify the types of your variables and functions, which can be useful in situations where the compiler is unable to infer the correct types or when you want to specify the types more explicitly for clarity or maintenance purposes. In general, you should use type inference whenever possible and only use type annotations when necessary. This will help you write more concise and maintainable TypeScript code.

THE "ANY" TYPE AND WHY IT SHOULD BE USED WITH CAUTION

Welcome to the "The 'any' Type and Why it Should be Used with Caution" section of our course "Learn TypeScript"! In this article, we will cover the "any" type in TypeScript and why it should be used with caution. By the end of this article, you should have a good understanding of the "any" type and how to use it effectively in your TypeScript programs.

What is the "any" Type?

The "any" type in TypeScript is a special type that can be used to denote that a variable or function can have any type. It is similar to the "object" type in other programming languages, but it is more flexible and can represent any type, including primitive types and complex types. For example:

```typescript
let x: any = 10; // x can have any type
x = "hello"; // x can now be a string
function add(a: any, b: any): any {
  return a + b;
}
let result = add(1, 2); // result can have any type
```

In this example, we are using the "any" type to disable type checking for the variables "x" and "result" and the function "add". This allows us to assign and return any type of value without generating a type error.

Why the "any" Type Should be Used with Caution

While the "any" type can be useful in certain situations, it should generally be used with caution in TypeScript. This is because it can lead to less predictable and less maintainable code if used excessively.

One reason to use the "any" type with caution is that it can make your code more prone to type errors. When you use the "any" type, you are essentially disabling type checking for that variable or function, which means that you are responsible for ensuring that the correct types are used. If you make a mistake and assign an incorrect type, you may not notice until runtime, when it is more difficult to fix.

Another reason to use the "any" type with caution is that it can make your code less maintainable. When you use the "any" type, you are giving up the benefits of type checking, which can help you catch errors and ensure that your code is correct. This can make it more difficult to understand and modify your code, as you will not have the same level of guidance from the TypeScript compiler.

In general, you should use the "any" type only when you have a specific reason to do so, such as when you need to disable type checking for a specific part of your code. In most cases, it is better to use the correct types for your variables and functions, as this will help you write more predictable and maintainable code.

How to Use the "any" Type Effectively

If you do need to use the "any" type in your TypeScript code, there are a few things you can do to ensure that you are using it effectively:

- Use the "any" type sparingly: Try to use the "any" type only when you have a specific reason to do so, and avoid using it excessively.
- Document your use of the "any" type: If you do need to use the "any" type, make sure to document your reason for doing so. This will help other developers understand your code and make it easier to maintain.
- Test your code thoroughly: If you are using the "any" type, it is especially important to test your code thoroughly to ensure that it is correct. This will help you catch any errors or issues that may not have been caught by the TypeScript compiler.

Conclusion

In conclusion, this article has covered the "any" type in TypeScript and why it should be used with caution. You should now have a good understanding of this type and how to use it effectively in your TypeScript programs. In future sections of our course, we will cover more advanced topics, such as interfaces and classes, and how to use them to write more structured and reusable TypeScript code.

Exercises

To review these concepts, we will go through a series of exercises designed to test your understanding and apply what you have learned.

What is the "any" type in TypeScript, and when should you use it?
Why should you use the "any" type with caution in TypeScript?
What are some tips for using the "any" type effectively in TypeScript?
Can you use the "any" type for variables and functions in TypeScript?
How does the "any" type compare to other types in TypeScript?

Solutions

What is the "any" type in TypeScript, and when should you use it?
The "any" type in TypeScript is a special type that can be used to denote that a variable or function can have any type. It is useful when you do not know the type of a value or when you want to disable type checking for a specific part of your code. However, it should generally be used with caution, as it can lead to less predictable and less maintainable code if used excessively.

Why should you use the "any" type with caution in TypeScript?

The "any" type should be used with caution in TypeScript because it can make your code more prone to type errors and less maintainable. When you use the "any" type, you are disabling type checking for that variable or function, which means that you are responsible for ensuring that the correct types are used. This can make it more difficult to catch errors and understand your code, and can make it more difficult to modify and maintain your code in the future.

What are some tips for using the "any" type effectively in TypeScript?
Some tips for using the "any" type effectively in TypeScript include:

- Use the "any" type sparingly: Try to use the "any" type only when you have a specific reason to do so, and avoid using it excessively.
- Document your use of the "any" type: If you do need to use the "any" type, make sure to document your reason for doing so. This will help other developers understand your code and make it easier to maintain.
- Test your code thoroughly: If you are using the "any" type, it is especially important to test your code thoroughly to ensure that it is correct. This will help you catch any errors or issues that may not have been caught by the TypeScript compiler.

Can you use the "any" type for variables and functions in TypeScript?
Yes, you can use the "any" type for variables and functions in TypeScript. To use the "any" type for a variable, you can specify it as the type annotation for the variable. For example:

```
let x: any = 10; // x can have any type
```

To use the "any" type for a function, you can specify it as the return type of the function. For example:

```
function add(a: any, b: any): any {
    return a + b;
}
```

How does the "any" type compare to other types in TypeScript?
The "any" type in TypeScript is more flexible than other types, as it can represent any type, including primitive types and complex types. This means that it can be used in place of any other type. However, it is generally a good idea to use the "any" type sparingly, as it can lead to less predictable and less maintainable code if used excessively. In most cases, it is better to use the correct types for your variables and functions, as this will help you write more predictable and maintainable code.

UNDERSTANDING THE DIFFERENCE BETWEEN INTERFACES AND CLASSES IN TYPESCRIPT

Welcome to the "Understanding the Difference Between Interfaces and Classes in TypeScript" section of our course "Learn TypeScript"! In this article, we will cover the differences between interfaces and classes in TypeScript, and how you can use them to write more structured and reusable code. By the end of this article, you should have a good understanding of these concepts and be able to use them effectively in your TypeScript programs.

Introduction to Interfaces

Interfaces in TypeScript are used to describe the shape of an object. They define a set of properties and methods that an object should have, but do not provide any implementation for those properties and methods. For example:

```
interface Point {
  x: number;
  y: number;
  distanceToOrigin(): number;
}
```

In this example, we have defined an interface called "Point" that has two properties, "x" and "y", and one method, "distanceToOrigin". The interface specifies that an object that implements this interface must have these properties and method, but does not specify how they should be implemented.

To use an interface, you can create a class or object that implements it. For example:

```
class CartesianPoint implements Point {
  x: number;
  y: number;
  constructor(x: number, y: number) {
    this.x = x;
```

```
  this.y = y;
}
distanceToOrigin() {
  return Math.sqrt(this.x * this.x + this.y * this.y);
}
}
```

In this example, we have defined a class called "CartesianPoint" that implements the "Point" interface. The class defines the properties and method specified in the interface and provides an implementation for them.

Introduction to Classes

Classes in TypeScript are used to define objects that have both state and behavior. They provide a way to organize and structure your code, and can be used to create objects with specific properties and methods. For example:

```
class Point {
  x: number;
  y: number;
  constructor(x: number, y: number) {
    this.x = x;
    this.y = y;
  }
  distanceToOrigin() {
    return Math.sqrt(this.x * this.x + this.y * this.y);
  }
}
```

In this example, we have defined a class called "Point" that has two properties, "x" and "y", and one method, "distanceToOrigin". The class defines the structure and behavior of the "Point" object, and provides an implementation for the properties and method.

To use a class, you can create an instance of the class using the "new" operator. For example:

```
let point = new Point(3, 4);
console.log(point.distanceToOrigin()); // Outputs: 5
```

In this example, we have created an instance of the "Point" class called "point", and called the "distanceToOrigin" method on it.

Differences Between Interfaces and Classes

While both interfaces and classes are used to define the structure and behavior of objects in TypeScript, they have some key differences:

- Implementation: Interfaces define the structure of an object, but do not provide any implementation. Classes, on the other hand, define both the structure and the implementation of an object.
- Inheritance: Classes can inherit from other classes, using the "extends" keyword. Interfaces, on the other hand, cannot inherit from other interfaces, but can extend multiple interfaces using the "extends" keyword.
- Modifiers: Classes can have different levels of accessibility, using the "public", "private", and "protected" modifiers. Interfaces, on the other hand, do not have any accessibility modifiers and all members are automatically public.

When to Use Interfaces vs Classes

So, when should you use interfaces vs classes in TypeScript? The answer depends on your specific needs and goals. Here are a few guidelines to help you decide:

- Use interfaces when you want to define the structure of an object, but do not need to provide any implementation. Interfaces are useful when you want to specify a contract that other classes or objects must adhere to.
- Use classes when you want to define both the structure and the implementation of an object. Classes are useful when you want to create objects with specific properties and methods that you can reuse in your code.
- Use inheritance when you want to create a class that is a specialized version of another class. Inheritance is useful when you want to share common code between classes, but also add some specific behavior or properties.
- Use interfaces when you want to extend multiple classes or interfaces. Interfaces are useful when you want to define a complex object that has multiple inheritance chains.

Conclusion

In conclusion, this article has covered the differences between interfaces and classes in TypeScript, and how you can use them to write more structured and reusable code. You should now have a good understanding of these concepts and be able to use them effectively in your TypeScript programs. In future sections of our course, we will cover more advanced topics, such as generics and decorators, and how to use them to write more powerful TypeScript code.

Exercises

To review these concepts, we will go through a series of exercises designed to test your understanding and apply what you have learned.

What is the main difference between interfaces and classes in TypeScript?
Can classes inherit from other classes in TypeScript?
Can interfaces extend other interfaces in TypeScript?
Can you use the "public", "private", and "protected" modifiers with interfaces in TypeScript?
When should you use interfaces vs classes in TypeScript?

Solutions

What is the main difference between interfaces and classes in TypeScript?
The main difference between interfaces and classes in TypeScript is that interfaces define the structure of an object, but do not provide any implementation, while classes define both the structure and the implementation of an object.

Can classes inherit from other classes in TypeScript?
Yes, classes can inherit from other classes in TypeScript using the "extends" keyword. For example:

```
class Point {
  x: number;
  y: number;
}
class CartesianPoint extends Point {
  // CartesianPoint inherits from Point
}
```

Can interfaces extend other interfaces in TypeScript?
Yes, interfaces can extend multiple other interfaces in TypeScript using the "extends" keyword. For example:

```
interface Point {
  x: number;
  y: number;
}
interface ThreeDimensionalPoint extends Point {
  z: number;
}
```

Can you use the "public", "private", and "protected" modifiers with interfaces in TypeScript?
No, you cannot use the "public", "private", and "protected" modifiers with interfaces in TypeScript. All members of an interface are automatically public.

When should you use interfaces vs classes in TypeScript?
You should use interfaces when you want to define the structure of an object, but do not need to provide any implementation. You should use classes when you want to define both the structure and the implementation of an object. You should use inheritance when you want to create a class that is a specialized version of another class. You should use interfaces when you want to extend multiple classes or interfaces.

It's important to keep in mind that these are general guidelines, and you may need to use a combination of interfaces and classes in your TypeScript code depending on your specific needs and goals. It's also worth noting that there are other language features, such as generics and decorators, that can help you write more powerful and flexible TypeScript code. We will cover these topics in future sections of our course.

DEFINING INTERFACES AND IMPLEMENTING THEM IN CLASSES

Welcome to the "Defining Interfaces and Implementing Them in Classes in TypeScript" section of our course "Learn TypeScript"! In this article, we will cover how to define interfaces and implement them in classes in TypeScript, and how you can use them to write more structured and reusable code. By the end of this article, you should have a good understanding of these concepts and be able to use them effectively in your TypeScript programs.

Introduction to Interfaces

Interfaces in TypeScript are used to describe the shape of an object. They define a set of properties and methods that an object should have, but do not provide any implementation for those properties and methods. For example:

```
interface Point {
  x: number;
  y: number;
  distanceToOrigin(): number;
}
```

In this example, we have defined an interface called "Point" that has two properties, "x" and "y", and one method, "distanceToOrigin". The interface specifies that an object that implements this interface must have these properties and method, but does not specify how they should be implemented.

To use an interface, you can create a class or object that implements it. For example:

```
class CartesianPoint implements Point {
  x: number;
  y: number;
  constructor(x: number, y: number) {
    this.x = x;
    this.y = y;
  }
  distanceToOrigin() {
    return Math.sqrt(this.x * this.x + this.y * this.y);
```

```
  }
}
```

In this example, we have defined a class called "CartesianPoint" that implements the "Point" interface. The class defines the properties and method specified in the interface and provides an implementation for them.

Implementing Multiple Interfaces

A class or object can implement multiple interfaces in TypeScript by separating them with a comma. For example:

```
interface Shape {
  area(): number;
}
interface Solid {
  volume(): number;
}
class Cube implements Shape, Solid {
  width: number;
  height: number;
  depth: number;
  constructor(width: number, height: number, depth: number) {
    this.width = width;
    this.height = height;
    this.depth = depth;
  }
  area() {
    return this.width * this.height * 6;
  }
  volume() {
    return this.width * this.height * this.depth;
  }
}
```

In this example, we have defined two interfaces, "Shape" and "Solid", and a class called "Cube" that implements both interfaces. The class defines the properties and methods specified in both interfaces and provides an implementation for them.

Extending Interfaces

Interfaces in TypeScript can extend other interfaces using the "extends" keyword. This allows you to define a new interface that includes all the members of the base interface, and can also add additional members of its own. For example:

```typescript
interface Point {
  x: number;
  y: number;
}
interface ThreeDimensionalPoint extends Point {
  z: number;
}
```

In this example, we have defined an interface called "ThreeDimensionalPoint" that extends the "Point" interface. The "ThreeDimensionalPoint" interface includes all the members of the "Point" interface, as well as an additional member called "z".

A class or object that implements the "ThreeDimensionalPoint" interface must implement all the members of both the "ThreeDimensionalPoint" and "Point" interfaces. For example:

```typescript
class CartesianPoint implements ThreeDimensionalPoint {
  x: number;
  y: number;
  z: number;
  constructor(x: number, y: number, z: number) {
    this.x = x;
    this.y = y;
    this.z = z;
  }
}
```

In this example, we have defined a class called "CartesianPoint" that implements the "ThreeDimensionalPoint" interface. The class defines all the properties specified in the "ThreeDimensionalPoint" and "Point" interfaces.

Optional Members

Interfaces in TypeScript can have optional members, which can be marked with a "?" symbol. This means that an object that implements the interface does not have to include these optional members. For example:

```typescript
interface Point {
  x: number;
  y: number;
  label?: string;
```

```
}
class CartesianPoint implements Point {
  x: number;
  y: number;
  constructor(x: number, y: number) {
    this.x = x;
    this.y = y;
  }
}
let point = new CartesianPoint(3, 4);
console.log(point.label); // Outputs: undefined
```

In this example, we have defined an interface called "Point" that has an optional member called "label". The class "CartesianPoint" implements the "Point" interface, but does not include the "label" property. When we create an instance of the "CartesianPoint" class and try to access the "label" property, it returns "undefined".

Readonly Members

Interfaces in TypeScript can have readonly members, which can be marked with the "readonly" keyword. This means that the value of these members can be set only once, either in the constructor or when the object is created. For example:

```
interface Point {
  readonly x: number;
  readonly y: number;
}
class CartesianPoint implements Point {
  readonly x: number;
  readonly y: number;
  constructor(x: number, y: number) {
    this.x = x;
    this.y = y;
  }
}
let point = new CartesianPoint(3, 4);
point.x = 5; // Error: Cannot assign to 'x' because it is a read-only property
```

In this example, we have defined an interface called "Point" that has two readonly members, "x" and "y". The class "CartesianPoint" implements the "Point" interface and defines the readonly properties. When we try to change the value of the "x" property on the "point" object, we get an error because it is a readonly property.

Readonly properties are useful when you want to prevent the value of a property from being changed after it has been set. This can be helpful for maintaining the integrity of your data and avoiding unintended side effects.

Conclusion

In conclusion, this article has covered how to define interfaces and implement them in classes in TypeScript, and how you can use them to write more structured and reusable code. You should now have a good understanding of these concepts and be able to use them effectively in your TypeScript programs. In future sections of our course, we will cover more advanced topics, such as generics and decorators, and how to use them to write more powerful TypeScript code.

Exercises

To review these concepts, we will go through a series of exercises designed to test your understanding and apply what you have learned.

Can a class or object implement multiple interfaces in TypeScript?
Can interfaces extend other interfaces in TypeScript?
How do you define an interface in TypeScript?
How do you implement an interface in a class or object in TypeScript?
Can an interface have optional members in TypeScript?

Solutions

Can a class or object implement multiple interfaces in TypeScript?
Yes, a class or object can implement multiple interfaces in TypeScript by separating them with a comma. For example:

```typescript
interface Shape {
  area(): number;
}

interface Solid {
  volume(): number;
}

class Cube implements Shape, Solid {
  // Cube implements Shape and Solid
}
```

Can interfaces extend other interfaces in TypeScript?
Yes, interfaces can extend other interfaces in TypeScript using the "extends" keyword. This allows

you to define a new interface that includes all the members of the base interface, and can also add additional members of its own. For example:

```typescript
interface Point {
  x: number;
  y: number;
}
interface ThreeDimensionalPoint extends Point {
  z: number;
}
```

How do you define an interface in TypeScript?

To define an interface in TypeScript, use the "interface" keyword followed by the name of the interface and a set of curly braces that contain the members of the interface. For example:

```typescript
interface Point {
  x: number;
  y: number;
  distanceToOrigin(): number;
}
```

How do you implement an interface in a class or object in TypeScript?

To implement an interface in a class or object in TypeScript, use the "implements" keyword followed by the name of the interface. Then, define the properties and methods specified in the interface and provide an implementation for them. For example:

```typescript
class CartesianPoint implements Point {
  x: number;
  y: number;
  constructor(x: number, y: number) {
    this.x = x;
    this.y = y;
  }
  distanceToOrigin() {
    return Math.sqrt(this.x * this.x + this.y * this.y);
  }
}
```

Can an interface have optional members in TypeScript?

Yes, an interface can have optional members in TypeScript by marking them with a "?" symbol. This means that an object that implements the interface does not have to include these optional members. For example:

```typescript
interface Point {
  x: number;
  y: number;
  label?: string;
}
```

EXTENDING INTERFACES AND CLASSES

Welcome to the "Extending Interfaces and Classes in TypeScript" section of our course "Learn TypeScript"! In this article, we will cover how to extend interfaces and classes in TypeScript, and how you can use these features to write more structured and reusable code. By the end of this article, you should have a good understanding of these concepts and be able to use them effectively in your TypeScript programs.

Introduction to Extending Interfaces

Interfaces in TypeScript can be extended using the "extends" keyword. This allows you to define a new interface that includes all the members of the base interface, and can also add additional members of its own. For example:

```
interface Point {
  x: number;
  y: number;
}
interface ThreeDimensionalPoint extends Point {
  z: number;
}
```

In this example, we have defined an interface called "ThreeDimensionalPoint" that extends the "Point" interface. The "ThreeDimensionalPoint" interface includes all the members of the "Point" interface, as well as an additional member called "z".

A class or object that implements the "ThreeDimensionalPoint" interface must implement all the members of both the "ThreeDimensionalPoint" and "Point" interfaces. For example:

```
class CartesianPoint implements ThreeDimensionalPoint {
  x: number;
  y: number;
  z: number;
  constructor(x: number, y: number, z: number) {
    this.x = x;
    this.y = y;
```

```
    this.z = z;
  }
}
```

In this example, we have defined a class called "CartesianPoint" that implements the "ThreeDimensionalPoint" interface. The class defines all the properties specified in the "ThreeDimensionalPoint" and "Point" interfaces.

Introduction to Extending Classes

Classes in TypeScript can also be extended using the "extends" keyword. This allows you to create a subclass that inherits the properties and methods of the base class, and can also define additional properties and methods of its own. For example:

```
class Shape {
  area(): number {
    return 0;
  }
}

class Rectangle extends Shape {
  width: number;
  height: number;
  constructor(width: number, height: number) {
    super();
    this.width = width;
    this.height = height;
  }
  area() {
    return this.width * this.height;
  }
}
```

In this example, we have defined a class called "Rectangle" that extends the "Shape" class. The "Rectangle" class defines an additional property called "width" and an additional method called "area" that calculates the area of the rectangle.

The "Rectangle" class also calls the "super()" method in the constructor, which calls the constructor of the base class. This is important because it allows the base class to initialize its own properties and set up any necessary state before the subclass starts working with those properties.

It's worth noting that the "extends" keyword can also be used to extend interfaces. For example, you could define an interface called "Shape" and then define a class called "Rectangle" that extends that interface.

Overriding Methods in Subclasses

When you create a subclass in TypeScript, you can override the methods of the base class by defining a method with the same name in the subclass. The subclass's implementation of the method will be used instead of the base class's implementation. For example:

```typescript
class Shape {
  area(): number {
    return 0;
  }
}
class Rectangle extends Shape {
  width: number;
  height: number;
  constructor(width: number, height: number) {
    super();
    this.width = width;
    this.height = height;
  }
  area() {
    return this.width * this.height;
  }
}
let rectangle = new Rectangle(10, 20);
console.log(rectangle.area()); // Outputs: 200
```

In this example, we have defined a "Rectangle" class that extends the "Shape" class and overrides the "area" method. When we call the "area" method on an instance of the "Rectangle" class, it uses the subclass's implementation of the method, which calculates the area of the rectangle using the width and height properties.

It's important to note that when you override a method in a subclass, you should ensure that the subclass's implementation of the method is compatible with the base class's implementation. For example, if the base class's method returns a number, the subclass's method should also return a number. This helps to maintain the integrity of your code and avoid runtime errors.

Abstract Classes

In TypeScript, you can define an abstract class using the "abstract" keyword. An abstract class is a class that cannot be instantiated directly, but can be subclassed. Abstract classes are useful when you want to define a base class that provides common functionality, but requires subclasses to provide specific implementations for certain methods.

For example, you might define an abstract "Shape" class that has an "area" method, but leave the implementation of the "area" method up to the subclasses. This allows you to define the general structure of a shape, while still allowing subclasses to define their own specific behavior.

To define an abstract method in an abstract class, use the "abstract" keyword followed by the name of the method and its signature. For example:

```typescript
abstract class Shape {
  abstract area(): number;
}
```

Subclasses of an abstract class must implement all the abstract methods of the base class. If a subclass does not implement an abstract method, it must also be marked as "abstract". For example:

```typescript
abstract class Shape {
  abstract area(): number;
}

class Rectangle extends Shape {
  width: number;
  height: number;
  constructor(width: number, height: number) {
    super();
    this.width = width;
    this.height = height;
  }
  area() {
    return this.width * this.height;
  }
}

abstract class ThreeDimensionalShape extends Shape {
  abstract volume(): number;
}
```

In this example, we have defined an abstract "ThreeDimensionalShape" class that extends the "Shape" class and adds an abstract "volume" method. Since the "ThreeDimensionalShape" class does not provide an implementation for the "volume" method, it must also be marked as "abstract".

It's worth noting that abstract classes can also have concrete methods, which are methods that have a complete implementation. Concrete methods can be called directly on an instance of an abstract class, while abstract methods must be implemented by subclasses.

Conclusion

In conclusion, this article has covered how to extend interfaces and classes in TypeScript, and how you can use these features to write more structured and reusable code. You should now have a good understanding of these concepts and be able to use them effectively in your TypeScript programs. In future sections of our course, we will cover more advanced topics, such as generics and decorators, and how to use them to write more powerful TypeScript code.

Exercises

To review these concepts, we will go through a series of exercises designed to test your understanding and apply what you have learned.

Can an abstract class have an abstract constructor in TypeScript?

Can an abstract class have concrete properties in TypeScript?

Can a class that extends an abstract class override an abstract method with a concrete method in TypeScript?

Can an abstract method have a default implementation in TypeScript?

Can an abstract class have a concrete constructor in TypeScript?

Solutions

Can an abstract class have an abstract constructor in TypeScript?

No, an abstract class cannot have an abstract constructor in TypeScript. The purpose of an abstract constructor is to enforce that a class must have a specific constructor, but abstract classes cannot be instantiated directly. Therefore, it does not make sense to define an abstract constructor for an abstract class.

Can an abstract class have concrete properties in TypeScript?

Yes, an abstract class can have concrete properties in TypeScript. Concrete properties are properties that have a fixed value, and can be accessed directly on an instance of the abstract class.

Can a class that extends an abstract class override an abstract method with a concrete method in TypeScript?

Yes, a class that extends an abstract class can override an abstract method with a concrete method in TypeScript. When you override a method in a subclass, you can provide a complete implementation for the method using the "concrete" syntax. For example:

```
abstract class Shape {
  abstract area(): number;
}
class Rectangle extends Shape {
  width: number;
  height: number;
  constructor(width: number, height: number) {
    super();
    this.width = width;
```

```
    this.height = height;
  }
  area() {
    return this.width * this.height;
  }
}
```

In this example, we have defined an abstract "Shape" class with an abstract "area" method, and a "Rectangle" class that extends the "Shape" class and overrides the "area" method with a concrete implementation.

Can an abstract method have a default implementation in TypeScript?

No, an abstract method cannot have a default implementation in TypeScript. The purpose of an abstract method is to define a contract that requires subclasses to provide their own implementation for the method. If an abstract method had a default implementation, it would defeat the purpose of the abstract method and make it less flexible.

Can an abstract class have a concrete constructor in TypeScript?

Yes, an abstract class can have a concrete constructor in TypeScript. A concrete constructor is a constructor that has a complete implementation, and can be called directly on an instance of the abstract class. For example:

```
abstract class Shape {
  abstract area(): number;
  constructor(public name: string) {}
}
class Rectangle extends Shape {
  width: number;
  height: number;
  constructor(name: string, width: number, height: number) {
    super(name);
    this.width = width;
    this.height = height;
  }
  area() {
    return this.width * this.height;
  }
}
```

In this example, we have defined an abstract "Shape" class with an abstract "area" method and a concrete constructor that takes a "name" parameter. The "Rectangle" class extends the "Shape" class and provides its own implementation of the "area" method, and also calls the "super()" method in the constructor to pass the "name" parameter to the base class.

ACCESS MODIFIERS (PUBLIC, PRIVATE, PROTECTED) IN TYPESCRIPT

Welcome to the "Access Modifiers in TypeScript" section of our course "Learn TypeScript"! In this article, we will cover the different access modifiers available in TypeScript and how you can use them to control the visibility and accessibility of class members. By the end of this article, you should have a good understanding of these concepts and be able to use them effectively in your TypeScript programs.

Introduction to Access Modifiers

In object-oriented programming, access modifiers are used to control the visibility and accessibility of class members (e.g. properties and methods). Access modifiers allow you to specify whether a class member is accessible from outside the class, or whether it is only accessible within the class or its subclasses.

TypeScript supports three access modifiers: "public", "private", and "protected". The "public" modifier makes a class member accessible from anywhere, the "private" modifier makes a class member only accessible within the class, and the "protected" modifier makes a class member accessible within the class and its subclasses.

Public Access Modifier

The "public" access modifier is the default access modifier for class members in TypeScript. If you don't specify an access modifier for a class member, it will be treated as "public" by default.

A "public" class member can be accessed from anywhere, including outside the class and its subclasses. For example:

```
class Point {
  public x: number;
  public y: number;
  constructor(x: number, y: number) {
    this.x = x;
    this.y = y;
  }
}
```

```
}
let point = new Point(10, 20);
console.log(point.x); // Outputs: 10
console.log(point.y); // Outputs: 20
```

In this example, we have defined a "Point" class with "public" x and y properties, and a constructor that initializes those properties. We can access the x and y properties from outside the "Point" class using the "." operator.

Private Access Modifier

The "private" access modifier makes a class member only accessible within the class. A "private" class member cannot be accessed from outside the class or, you can use the "protected" access modifier to make a class member accessible within the class and its subclasses.

For example:

```
class Shape {
 protected area: number;
 constructor(area: number) {
  this.area = area;
 }
}
class Rectangle extends Shape {
 width: number;
 height: number;
 constructor(width: number, height: number) {
  super(width * height);
  this.width = width;
  this.height = height;
 }
 getArea() {
  return this.area;
 }
}
let rectangle = new Rectangle(10, 20);
console.log(rectangle.getArea()); // Outputs: 200
```

In this example, we have defined a "Shape" class with a "protected" "area" property and a constructor that initializes the "area" property. We have also defined a "Rectangle" class that extends the "Shape" class and has a "getArea" method that returns the "area" property. Since the "area" property is "protected", it is only accessible within the "Shape" class and its subclasses (i.e. the "Rectangle" class).

Conclusion

In conclusion, this article has covered the different access modifiers available in TypeScript and how you can use them to control the visibility and accessibility of class members. You should now have a good understanding of these concepts and be able to use them effectively in your TypeScript programs. In future sections of our course, we will cover more advanced topics, such as generics and decorators, and how to use them to write more powerful TypeScript code.

Exercises

To review these concepts, we will go through a series of exercises designed to test your understanding and apply what you have learned.

Can a "private" class member be accessed from outside the class in TypeScript?
Can a "protected" class member be accessed from outside the class in TypeScript?
Can a "public" class member be accessed from within a subclass in TypeScript?
Can a "private" class member be accessed from within a subclass in TypeScript?
Can a "protected" class member be accessed from within a subclass in TypeScript?

Solutions

Can a "private" class member be accessed from outside the class in TypeScript?
No, a "private" class member cannot be accessed from outside the class in TypeScript. The "private" access modifier makes a class member only accessible within the class, and it cannot be accessed from outside the class or its subclasses.

Can a "protected" class member be accessed from outside the class in TypeScript?
No, a "protected" class member cannot be accessed from outside the class in TypeScript. The "protected" access modifier makes a class member only accessible within the class and its subclasses, and it cannot be accessed from outside the class or its subclasses.

Can a "public" class member be accessed from within a subclass in TypeScript?
Yes, a "public" class member can be accessed from within a subclass in TypeScript. The "public" access modifier makes a class member accessible from anywhere, including within the class and its subclasses.

Can a "private" class member be accessed from within a subclass in TypeScript?
No, a "private" class member cannot be accessed from within a subclass in TypeScript. The "private" access modifier makes a class member only accessible within the class, and it cannot be accessed from outside the class or its subclasses.

Can a "protected" class member be accessed from within a subclass in TypeScript?
Yes, a "protected" class member can be accessed from within a subclass in TypeScript. The "protected" access modifier makes a class member accessible within the class and its subclasses, so it can be accessed from within a subclass.

However, it is important to note that a "protected" class member cannot be accessed from outside the class or its subclasses. It is only accessible within the class and its subclasses, and it is not accessible from any other context.

For example:

```
class Shape {
 protected area: number;
 constructor(area: number) {
  this.area = area;
 }
}
class Rectangle extends Shape {
 width: number;
 height: number;
 constructor(width: number, height: number) {
  super(width * height);
  this.width = width;
  this.height = height;
 }
 getArea() {
  return this.area; // Accessing protected property from within subclass
 }
}
let rectangle = new Rectangle(10, 20);
console.log(rectangle.getArea()); // Outputs: 200
console.log(rectangle.area); // Compiler error: Property 'area' is protected and only accessible within class 'Shape' and its subclasses.
```

In this example, we have defined a "Shape" class with a "protected" "area" property and a constructor that initializes the "area" property. We have also defined a "Rectangle" class that extends the "Shape" class and has a "getArea" method that returns the "area" property. Since the "area" property is "protected", it is only accessible within the "Shape" class and its subclasses (i.e. the "Rectangle" class).

If we try to access the "area" property from outside the "Rectangle" class, we will get a compiler error because the "area" property is "protected" and not "public". This is to ensure that "protected" class members are only accessible within the class and its subclasses, and not from any other context.

DECLARING FUNCTIONS
IN TYPESCRIPT

Welcome to the "Declaring Functions in TypeScript" section of our course "Learn TypeScript"! In this article, we will cover the different ways to declare functions in TypeScript and how you can use them to write clean and efficient code. By the end of this article, you should have a good understanding of these concepts and be able to use them effectively in your TypeScript programs.

Introduction to Functions

In TypeScript (and in many programming languages), a function is a block of code that performs a specific task. Functions can take input parameters, perform some operations using those parameters, and return a result.

For example, we can define a simple function that adds two numbers:

```typescript
function add(x: number, y: number): number {
  return x + y;
}
console.log(add(10, 20)); // Outputs: 30
```

In this example, we have defined a function named "add" that takes two input parameters (x and y) of type "number" and returns a result of type "number". We can call the "add" function by passing it two arguments (10 and 20), and it will return the sum of those numbers (30).

Function Declarations

The most common way to declare a function in TypeScript is using a function declaration. A function declaration consists of the "function" keyword, followed by the function name, a list of parameters, and a function body.

For example:

```typescript
function add(x: number, y: number): number {
  return x + y;
}
```

In this example, we have defined a function named "add" that takes two input parameters (x and y) of type "number" and returns a result of type "number". The function body consists of a single return statement that adds the x and y parameters and returns the result.

Function Declarations vs Function Expressions

It is important to note that function declarations and function expressions are not interchangeable in TypeScript. Function declarations are hoisted (i.e. they are moved to the top of the script at runtime), while function expressions are not. This means that you can call a function declaration before it is defined in the script, but you cannot do the same with a function expression.

For example:

```
// Function declaration
function add(x: number, y: number): number {
  return x + y;
}
console.log(add(10, 20)); // Outputs: 30
// Function expression
let subtract = function(x: number, y: number): number {
  return x - y;
};
console.log(subtract(10, 20)); // Outputs: -10
```

In this example, we have defined a function declaration named "add" and a function expression named "subtract". We can call the "add" function before it is defined in the script, but we cannot do the same with the "subtract" function because it is a function expression.

Arrow Functions

Arrow functions (also known as "lambda functions") are a shorthand syntax for defining functions in TypeScript. They are especially useful when you want to define a simple function with a single statement.

For example:

```
let add = (x: number, y: number) => x + y;
```

In this example, we have defined an arrow function named "add" that takes two input parameters (x and y) of type "number" and returns the sum of those numbers. The "=>" operator separates the input parameters from the function body.

You can also specify the return type of an arrow function using a type annotation. For example:

```
let add: (x: number, y: number) => number =
(x, y) => x + y;
```

In this example, we have used a type annotation to specify that the "add" function takes two input parameters (x and y) of type "number" and returns a result of type "number".

If you need to define a function with a block body (i.e. a function with multiple statements), you can use curly braces to enclose the function body and a "return" statement to specify the function's return value. For example:

```typescript
let add = (x: number, y: number): number => {
  let result = x + y;
  return result;
};
```

In this example, we have defined an arrow function named "add" that takes two input parameters (x and y) of type "number" and returns the sum of those numbers. The function body consists of a single "let" statement that declares a variable named "result" and assigns it the value of the x and y parameters. The function returns the "result" variable.

Optional and Default Parameters

In TypeScript, you can specify optional parameters by adding a "?" character after the parameter name. Optional parameters are parameters that are not required to be passed to the function when it is called.

For example:

```typescript
function greet(name: string, greeting?: string): void {
  console.log(`Hello, ${name}! ${greeting || "}`);
}

greet('John'); // Outputs: "Hello, John!"
greet('John', 'How are you doing?'); // Outputs: "Hello, John! How are you doing?"
```

In this example, we have defined a function named "greet" that takes two parameters: a required "name" parameter of type "string" and an optional "greeting" parameter of type "string". If the "greeting" parameter is not passed to the function, it will default to an empty string.

You can also specify default values for parameters in TypeScript using the "=" operator. Default values are values that are assigned to the parameter if it is not passed to the function when it is called.

For example:

```typescript
function greet(name: string, greeting: string = 'Hi'): void {
  console.log(`Hello, ${name}! ${greeting}`);
}

greet('John'); // Outputs: "Hello, John! Hi"
greet('John', 'How are you doing?'); // Outputs: "Hello, John! How are you doing?"
```

In this example, we have defined a function named "greet" that takes two parameters: a required "name" parameter of type "string" and a "greeting" parameter of type "string" with a default value of "Hi". If the "greeting" parameter is not passed to the function, it will default to "Hi".

You can also use default values in combination with optional parameters in TypeScript. For example:

```typescript
function greet(name: string, greeting?: string, punctuation: string = '!'): void {
  console.log(`Hello, ${name}! ${greeting || ''}${punctuation}`);
}

greet('John'); // Outputs: "Hello, John!"
greet('John', 'How are you doing?'); // Outputs: "Hello, John! How are you doing?"
greet('John', undefined, '...'); // Outputs: "Hello, John! ..."
```

In this example, we have defined a function named "greet" that takes three parameters: a required "name" parameter of type "string", an optional "greeting" parameter of type "string", and a "punctuation" parameter of type "string" with a default value of "!". If the "greeting" parameter is not passed to the function, it will default to an empty string. If the "punctuation" parameter is not passed to the function, it will default to "!".

Rest Parameters

In TypeScript, you can use rest parameters to specify a variable number of arguments in a function. Rest parameters are specified using the "…" operator followed by the parameter name.

For example:

```typescript
function add(...numbers: number[]): number {
  let result = 0;
  for (const number of numbers) {
    result += number;
  }
  return result;
}
console.log(add(1, 2, 3, 4, 5)); // Outputs: 15
```

In this example, we have defined a function named "add" that takes a variable number of arguments of type "number". The "numbers" parameter is a rest parameter that represents an array of numbers. The function body iterates over the "numbers" array using a "for...of" loop and adds up all the numbers using a variable named "result". Finally, the function returns the "result" variable.

You can use rest parameters in combination with other parameters in TypeScript. For example:

```typescript
function greet(greeting: string, ...names: string[]): void {
  for (const name of names) {
    console.log(`${greeting}, ${name}!`);
  }
}
greet('Hello', 'John', 'Jane', 'Bob');
```

```
// Outputs: "Hello, John!"
//         "Hello, Jane!"
//         "Hello, Bob!"
```

In this example, we have defined a function named "greet" that takes a required "greeting" parameter of type "string" and a variable number of "names" parameters of type "string[]". The function body iterates over the "names" array using a "for...of" loop and prints a greeting for each name.

Overloads

In TypeScript, you can use function overloading to define multiple functions with the same name but different signatures. Function overloading allows you to define multiple functions with different parameter lists and return types.

For example:

```
function greet(name: string): string;
function greet(age: number): string;
function greet(value: string | number): string {
 if (typeof value === 'string') {
  return `Hello, ${value}!`;
 } else {
  return `You are ${value} years old.`;
 }
}
console.log(greet('John')); // Outputs: "Hello, John!"
console.log(greet(30)); // Outputs: "You are 30 years old."
```

In this example, we have defined a function named "greet" that has two overloads: one that takes a "name" parameter of type "string" and returns a "string", and another that takes an "age" parameter of type "number" and returns a "string". The implementation of the "greet" function uses a type guard to determine the type of the "value" parameter and returns a different string depending on the type.

Function overloading is a powerful feature that allows you to provide different implementations of a function depending on the type of the input parameters. It is especially useful when you want to provide different behaviors for different types of input.

Conclusion

In this article, we have covered the different ways to declare functions in TypeScript and how you can use them to write clean and efficient code. We have learned about function declarations, function expressions, arrow functions, optional and default parameters, rest parameters, and function overloading.

By now, you should have a good understanding of these concepts and be able to use them effectively in your TypeScript programs. We hope you found this article helpful and that you will continue learning about TypeScript and all the other features it has to offer.

Exercises

To review these concepts, we will go through a series of exercises designed to test your understanding and apply what you have learned.

Declare a function named "greet" that takes a single parameter "name" of type "string" and returns a string in the following format: "Hello, [name]!".

Declare a function named "add" that takes two parameters "x" and "y" of type "number" and returns the sum of those numbers. Use an arrow function to define the function.

Declare a function named "greet" that takes a single optional parameter "greeting" of type "string" with a default value of "Hi". The function should return a string in the following format: "Hello, [greeting]!". Use a type annotation to specify the return type of the function.

Declare a function named "add" that takes a variable number of arguments of type "number" and returns the sum of those numbers. Use a rest parameter to specify the variable number of arguments.

Declare a function named "greet" that has two overloads: one that takes a single parameter "name" of type "string" and returns a "string", and another that takes a single parameter "age" of type "number" and returns a "string". Use function overloading to define the two overloads and provide an implementation that returns different strings depending on the type of the input parameter.

Solutions

Declare a function named "greet" that takes a single parameter "name" of type "string" and returns a string in the following format: "Hello, [name]!".

```
function greet(name: string): string {
  return `Hello, ${name}!`;
}
console.log(greet('John')); // Outputs: "Hello, John!"
```

Declare a function named "add" that takes two parameters "x" and "y" of type "number" and returns the sum of those numbers. Use an arrow function to define the function.

```
let add = (x: number, y: number) => x + y;
console.log(add(1, 2)); // Outputs: 3
```

Declare a function named "greet" that takes a single optional parameter "greeting" of type "string" with a default value of "Hi". The function should return a string in the following format: "Hello, [greeting]!". Use a type annotation to specify the return type of the function.

```typescript
function greet(greeting: string = 'Hi'): string {
  return `Hello, ${greeting}!`;
}
console.log(greet()); // Outputs: "Hello, Hi!"
console.log(greet('How are you doing?')); // Outputs: "Hello, How are you doing?"
```

Declare a function named "add" that takes a variable number of arguments of type "number" and returns the sum of those numbers. Use a rest parameter to specify the variable number of arguments.

```typescript
function add(...numbers: number[]): number {
  let result = 0;
  for (const number of numbers) {
    result += number;
  }
  return result;
}
console.log(add(1, 2, 3, 4, 5)); // Outputs: 15
```

Declare a function named "greet" that has two overloads: one that takes a single parameter "name" of type "string" and returns a "string", and another that takes a single parameter "age" of type "number" and returns a "string". Use function overloading to define the two overloads and provide an implementation that returns different strings depending on the type of the input parameter.

```typescript
function greet(name: string): string;
function greet(age: number): string;
function greet(value: string | number): string {
  if (typeof value === 'string') {
    return `Hello, ${value}!`;
  } else {
    return `You are ${value} years old.`;
  }
}
console.log(greet('John')); // Outputs: "Hello, John!"
console.log(greet(30)); // Outputs: "You are 30 years old."
```

FUNCTION RETURN TYPES AND PARAMETER TYPES

In TypeScript, you can specify the return type of a function using a type annotation. The return type specifies the data type of the value returned by the function.

For example:

```
function greet(name: string): string {
  return `Hello, ${name}!`;
}
console.log(greet('John')); // Outputs: "Hello, John!"
```

In this example, we have defined a function named "greet" that takes a single parameter "name" of type "string" and returns a "string". We have specified the return type of the function using the ": string" type annotation after the parameter list.

You can also specify the return type using the "void" type to indicate that the function does not return a value. For example:

```
function printGreeting(name: string): void {
  console.log(`Hello, ${name}!`);
}
printGreeting('John'); // Outputs: "Hello, John!"
```

In this example, we have defined a function named "printGreeting" that takes a single parameter "name" of type "string" and returns "void". The function body logs a greeting to the console but does not return a value.

Function Parameter Types

In TypeScript, you can specify the type of each parameter in a function using a type annotation. The parameter type specifies the data type of the value passed to the function as an argument.

For example:

```
function greet(name: string): string {
  return `Hello, ${name}!`;
}
```

```
console.log(greet('John')); // Outputs: "Hello, John!"
```

In this example, we have defined a function named "greet" that takes a single parameter "name" of type "string". The "name" parameter must be passed a value of type "string" when the function is called.

You can specify multiple parameters in a function, each with its own type annotation. For example:

```
function add(x: number, y: number): number {
  return x + y;
}
console.log(add(1, 2)); // Outputs: 3
```

In this example, we have defined a function named "add" that takes two parameters "x" and "y" of type "number". The "x" and "y" parameters must be passed values of type "number" when the function is called. The function returns the sum of "x" and "y".

Optional Parameters

Optional parameters are a useful feature in TypeScript as they allow you to define a function with parameters that are not always required. This can be useful when you want to provide default values for certain parameters or when you want to allow the caller to choose which parameters to specify.

For example:

```
function greet(name: string, greeting?: string): string {
  return `${greeting || 'Hi'}, ${name}!`;
}
console.log(greet('John')); // Outputs: "Hi, John!"
console.log(greet('John', 'How are you doing')); // Outputs: "How are you doing, John!"
```

In this example, we have defined a function named "greet" that takes a single required parameter "name" of type "string" and an optional parameter "greeting" of type "string". If the "greeting" parameter is not specified when the function is called, the default value of "Hi" is used.

You can also specify default values for optional parameters using the "= defaultValue" syntax. For example:

```
function greet(name: string, greeting: string = 'Hi'): string {
  return `${greeting}, ${name}!`;
}
console.log(greet('John')); // Outputs: "Hi, John!"
console.log(greet('John', 'How are you doing')); // Outputs: "How are you doing, John!"
```

In this example, we have defined a function named "greet" that takes a single required parameter "name" of type "string" and an optional parameter "greeting" of type "string" with a default value of "Hi". If the "greeting" parameter is not specified when the function is called, the default value of "Hi" is used.

Rest Parameters

In TypeScript, you can use a rest parameter to specify a variable number of arguments in a function. The rest parameter is defined using the "..." syntax and must be the last parameter in the function's parameter list.

For example:

```typescript
function add(...numbers: number[]): number {
  let result = 0;
  for (const number of numbers) {
    result += number;
  }
  return result;
}
console.log(add(1, 2, 3, 4, 5)); // Outputs: 15
```

In this example, we have defined a function named "add" that takes a variable number of arguments of type "number" and returns the sum of those numbers. The "numbers" parameter is defined as a rest parameter using the "..." syntax and is of type "number[]". The function uses a loop to iterate over the "numbers" array and adds each number to the "result" variable.

Function Overloading

Function overloading is a useful feature in TypeScript as it allows you to define multiple versions of a function that can be called with different argument types. This can be useful when you want to provide different implementations of a function based on the type of the arguments.

For example:

```typescript
function greet(name: string): string;
function greet(age: number): string;
function greet(value: string | number): string {
  if (typeof value === 'string') {
    return `Hello, ${value}!`;
  } else {
    return `You are ${value} years old`;
  }
}
console.log(greet('John')); // Outputs: "Hello, John!"
console.log(greet(30)); // Outputs: "You are 30 years old"
```

In this example, we have defined a function named "greet" that has three declarations. The first declaration specifies a single parameter "name" of type "string" and a return type of "string". The second declaration specifies a single parameter "age" of type "number" and a return type of "string". The third declaration specifies a single parameter "value" of type "string" or "number" and a return type of "string".

The function body contains a conditional statement that checks the type of the "value" parameter and returns a different greeting based on the type. If "value" is of type "string", the function returns a greeting using the "name" parameter. If "value" is of type "number", the function returns a greeting using the "age" parameter.

You can call the "greet" function with either a "string" or a "number" argument and the correct version of the function will be called based on the type of the argument.

Conclusion

In conclusion, function return types and parameter types are an important aspect of TypeScript programming. They allow you to specify the data types of function arguments and return values, as well as provide optional and rest parameters and use function overloading. Understanding and properly using these features will help you write more reliable and maintainable code in your TypeScript projects.

Exercises

To review these concepts, we will go through a series of exercises designed to test your understanding and apply what you have learned.

Write a function named "sum" that takes an array of numbers and returns the sum of those numbers. Use a type annotation to specify the parameter and return types.

Write a function named "greet" that takes a string and an optional boolean parameter and returns a greeting based on the string and boolean value. Use type annotations to specify the parameter and return types.

Write a function named "calculateSum" that takes a variable number of numbers and returns the sum of those numbers. Use a rest parameter and a type annotation to specify the parameter and return types.

Write a function named "greetPerson" that takes a string and returns a greeting based on the string. Use function overloading and type annotations to specify the parameter and return types.

Write a class named "Person" that has three private properties: "name", "age", and "phoneNumber". Add getters and setters for each property and use type annotations to specify the types.

Solutions

Write a function named "sum" that takes an array of numbers and returns the sum of those numbers. Use a type annotation to specify the parameter and return types.

```
function sum(numbers: number[]): number {
    let result = 0;
```

```
for (const number of numbers) {
  result += number;
}
return result;
}
console.log(sum([1, 2, 3, 4, 5])); // Outputs: 15
```

Write a function named "greet" that takes a string and an optional boolean parameter and returns a greeting based on the string and boolean value. Use type annotations to specify the parameter and return types.

```
function greet(name: string, isFormal: boolean = false): string {
  if (isFormal) {
    return `Hello, ${name}!`;
  } else {
    return `Hi, ${name}!`;
  }
}
console.log(greet('John')); // Outputs: "Hi, John!"
console.log(greet('John', true)); // Outputs: "Hello, John!"
```

Write a function named "calculateSum" that takes a variable number of numbers and returns the sum of those numbers. Use a rest parameter and a type annotation to specify the parameter and return types.

```
function calculateSum(...numbers: number[]): number {
  let result = 0;
  for (const number of numbers) {
    result += number;
  }
  return result;
}
console.log(calculateSum(1, 2, 3, 4, 5)); // Outputs: 15
```

Write a function named "greetPerson" that takes a string and returns a greeting based on the string. Use function overloading and type annotations to specify the parameter and return types.

```
function greetPerson(name: string): string;
function greetPerson(age: number): string;
function greetPerson(value: string | number): string {
  if (typeof value === 'string') {
    return `Hello, ${value}!`;
```

```
  } else {
    return `You are ${value} years old`;
  }
}
console.log(greetPerson('John')); // Outputs: "Hello, John!"
console.log(greetPerson(30)); // Outputs: "You are 30 years old"
```

Write a class named "Person" that has three private properties: "name", "age", and "phoneNumber". Add getters and setters for each property and use type annotations to specify the types.

```
class Person {
  private _name: string;
  private _age: number;
  private _phoneNumber: string;
  get name(): string {
    return this._name;
  }
  set name(value: string) {
    this._name = value;
  }
  get age(): number {
    return this._age;
  }
  set age(value: number) {
    this._age = value;
  }
  get phoneNumber(): string {
    return this._phoneNumber;
  }
  set phoneNumber(value: string) {
    this._phoneNumber = value;
  }
}
const person = new Person();
person.name = 'John';
person.age = 30;
person.phoneNumber = '123-456-7890';
```

```
console.log(person.name); // Outputs: "John"
console.log(person.age); // Outputs: 30
console.log(person.phoneNumber); // Outputs: "123-456-7890"
```

OPTIONAL AND DEFAULT PARAMETERS IN TYPESCRIPT FUNCTIONS

In TypeScript, optional and default parameters allow you to specify parameters in a function declaration that are not required to be passed when the function is called. This can be useful when you want to provide default values for parameters or allow the caller to omit certain parameters.

Optional Parameters:

To declare an optional parameter in a function, you can use the "?" symbol after the parameter name. For example:

```
function greet(name?: string): string {
  return `Hello, ${name || 'there'}!`;
}

console.log(greet()); // Outputs: "Hello, there!"
console.log(greet('John')); // Outputs: "Hello, John!"
```

In this example, the "name" parameter is declared as an optional parameter using the "?" symbol. The function body uses the "||" operator to provide a default value of "there" if the "name" parameter is not provided.

You can also specify multiple optional parameters in a function declaration by using the "?" symbol after each parameter name. For example:

```
function greet(firstName?: string, lastName?: string): string {
  return `Hello, ${firstName || 'there'} ${lastName || ''}!`;
}

console.log(greet()); // Outputs: "Hello, there!"
console.log(greet('John')); // Outputs: "Hello, John!"
console.log(greet('John', 'Doe')); // Outputs: "Hello, John Doe!"
```

In this example, the "firstName" and "lastName" parameters are both declared as optional parameters using the "?" symbol. The function body uses the "||" operator to provide default values for each parameter if they are not provided.

Default Parameters:

In addition to optional parameters, TypeScript also supports default parameters. Default parameters allow you to specify a default value for a parameter in the function declaration that will be used if the parameter is not provided when the function is called.

To declare a default parameter, you can use the "=" symbol followed by the default value after the parameter name. For example:

```typescript
function greet(name: string = 'there'): string {
  return `Hello, ${name}!`;
}
console.log(greet()); // Outputs: "Hello, there!"
console.log(greet('John')); // Outputs: "Hello, John!"
```

In this example, the "name" parameter is declared with a default value of "there" using the "=" symbol. If the "name" parameter is not provided when the function is called, the default value will be used. If the "name" parameter is provided, the default value will be overridden.

You can also specify multiple default parameters in a function declaration by using the "=" symbol followed by the default value after each parameter name. For example:

```typescript
function greet(firstName: string = 'there', lastName: string = ''): string {
  return `Hello, ${firstName} ${lastName}!`;
}
console.log(greet()); // Outputs: "Hello, there!"
console.log(greet('John')); // Outputs: "Hello, John!"
console.log(greet('John', 'Doe')); // Outputs: "Hello, John Doe!"
```

In this example, the "firstName" and "lastName" parameters are both declared with default values using the "=" symbol. If either parameter is not provided when the function is called, the default value will be used. If either parameter is provided, the default value will be overridden.

Why Should You Use Optional and Default Parameters?

Optional and default parameters can be useful in a number of situations. For example:

- Providing default values for parameters can make it easier for the caller to use the function, as they don't have to provide every parameter every time.
- Using optional parameters can make it easier to add new functionality to a function without breaking existing code that calls the function.
- Optional and default parameters can help reduce the number of overloads required for a function, as you can use optional and default parameters to handle a range of possible parameter combinations.

Conclusion

In this article, we learned about optional and default parameters in TypeScript. We saw how to use the "?" symbol to declare optional parameters and the "=" symbol to declare default parameters. We also looked at some of the benefits of using optional and default parameters in your code. Understanding how to use optional and default parameters can help you write more flexible and reusable code in your TypeScript projects.

Exercises

To review these concepts, we will go through a series of exercises designed to test your understanding and apply what you have learned.

Write a function named "greet" that takes an optional parameter "name" and returns a greeting based on the value of "name". Use an optional parameter and a default value to specify the parameter.

Write a function named "addNumbers" that takes two optional parameters "x" and "y" and returns the sum of the two numbers. Use optional parameters and default values to specify the parameters.

Write a class named "Person" that has three private properties: "name", "age", and "phoneNumber". Add getters and setters for each property and use default values to specify the default values for the "age" and "phoneNumber" properties.

Write a function named "formatPhoneNumber" that takes a string parameter "phoneNumber" and returns the phone number in a standardized format. Use a default value to specify the default value for the "phoneNumber" parameter.

Write a function named "calculateTotal" that takes two optional parameters "price" and "quantity" and returns the total cost of the purchase. Use optional parameters and default values to specify the parameters.

Solutions

Write a function named "greet" that takes an optional parameter "name" and returns a greeting based on the value of "name". Use an optional parameter and a default value to specify the parameter.

```typescript
function greet(name: string = 'there'): string {
  return `Hello, ${name}!`;
}
console.log(greet()); // Outputs: "Hello, there!"
console.log(greet('John')); // Outputs: "Hello, John!"
```

Write a function named "addNumbers" that takes two optional parameters "x" and "y" and returns the sum of the two numbers. Use optional parameters and default values to specify the parameters.

```typescript
function addNumbers(x: number = 0, y: number = 0): number {
  return x + y;
}
console.log(addNumbers()); // Outputs: 0
```

```
console.log(addNumbers(1)); // Outputs: 1
```
```
console.log(addNumbers(1, 2)); // Outputs: 3
```

Write a class named "Person" that has three private properties: "name", "age", and "phoneNumber". Add getters and setters for each property and use default values to specify the default values for the "age" and "phoneNumber" properties.

```
class Person {
  private _name: string;
  private _age: number = 0;
  private _phoneNumber: string = '';
  get name(): string {
    return this._name;
  }
  set name(value: string) {
    this._name = value;
  }
  get age(): number {
    return this._age;
  }
  set age(value: number) {
    this._age = value;
  }
  get phoneNumber(): string {
    return this._phoneNumber;
  }
  set phoneNumber(value: string) {
    this._phoneNumber = value;
  }
}
class Person {
  // your code here
}
const person = new Person();
person.name = 'John';
console.log(person.name); // Outputs: "John"
console.log(person.age); // Outputs: 0
console.log(person.phoneNumber); // Outputs: ""
```

Write a function named "formatPhoneNumber" that takes a string parameter "phoneNumber" and returns the phone number in a standardized format. Use a default value to specify the default value for the "phoneNumber" parameter.

```typescript
function formatPhoneNumber(phoneNumber: string = '123-456-7890'): string {
  const formattedPhoneNumber = phoneNumber.replace(/(\d{3})(\d{3})(\d{4})/, '$1-$2-$3');
  return formattedPhoneNumber;
}
console.log(formatPhoneNumber()); // Outputs: "123-456-7890"
console.log(formatPhoneNumber('1234567890')); // Outputs: "123-456-7890"
```

Write a function named "calculateTotal" that takes two optional parameters "price" and "quantity" and returns the total cost of the purchase. Use optional parameters and default values to specify the parameters.

```typescript
function calculateTotal(price: number = 0, quantity: number = 1): number {
  return price * quantity;
}
console.log(calculateTotal()); // Outputs: 0
console.log(calculateTotal(10)); // Outputs: 10
console.log(calculateTotal(10, 2)); // Outputs: 20
```

REST PARAMETERS IN TYPESCRIPT FUNCTIONS

In Typescript, rest parameters allow you to represent an indefinite number of arguments as an array. This is useful when you don't know in advance how many arguments a function will receive, or when you want to pass a variable number of arguments to another function. In this article, we'll take a closer look at how to use rest parameters in Typescript functions.

What are Rest Parameters?

Rest parameters are a way to represent an indefinite number of arguments as an array. They are denoted by three dots (...) followed by the name of the array that will hold the arguments. For example:

```typescript
function sum(...numbers: number[]): number {
  let total = 0;
  for (const number of numbers) {
    total += number;
  }
  return total;
}
```

In the above example, the function "sum" takes an indefinite number of arguments of type "number" and stores them in an array named "numbers".

It's important to note that rest parameters must be the last parameter in a function's parameter list. This is because the rest parameter collects all remaining arguments into an array. If there are any other parameters after the rest parameter, they will not be included in the array.

Using Rest Parameters in Typescript Functions

Now that we've seen how to declare a rest parameter, let's look at some examples of how to use it in a Typescript function.

One common use case for rest parameters is to pass a variable number of arguments to another function. For example, let's say we have a function that logs messages to the console:

```typescript
function log(message: string, ...values: any[]) {
  console.log(message, ...values);
```

```
}
```

In this example, the "log" function takes a message string as its first argument and an indefinite number of additional arguments as a rest parameter. The rest parameter is then spread using the spread operator (…) when the message and values are logged to the console.

This allows us to pass a variable number of arguments to the "log" function, like this:

```
log('Hello, world!'); // Outputs: "Hello, world!"
```

```
log('The value of x is:', x); // Outputs: "The value of x is: 10"
```

```
log('The values of x and y are:', x, y); // Outputs: "The values of x and y are: 10 20"
```

Another use case for rest parameters is to perform calculations on a variable number of arguments. For example, let's say we want to write a function that calculates the average of a given set of numbers:

```
function average(...numbers: number[]): number {
  let total = 0;
  for (const number of numbers) {
    total += number;
  }
  return total / numbers.length;
}
```

In this example, the "average" function takes an indefinite number of numbers as a rest parameter and calculates their average by summing the numbers and dividing by the length of the array.

This allows us to pass a variable number of arguments to the "average" function and calculate their average, like this:

```
console.log(average(1, 2, 3, 4, 5)); // Outputs: 3
```

```
console.log(average(1, 3, 5, 7, 9)); // Outputs: 5
```

```
console.log(average(10, 20, 30)); // Outputs: 20
```

Rest Parameters and Type Inference

In Typescript, the type of the rest parameter is inferred from the arguments that are passed to the function. For example:

```
function printValues(...values: any[]) {
  console.log(values);
}
printValues(1, 'hello', true); // Outputs: [1, 'hello', true]
```

In this example, the "printValues" function takes an indefinite number of arguments and stores them in an array of type "any". Since we passed a number, a string, and a boolean to the function, the rest parameter is inferred to be of type "any[]".

If we want to specify a more specific type for the rest parameter, we can do so by annotating the parameter with the desired type. For example:

```
function printNumbers(...numbers: number[]) {
  console.log(numbers);
}
printNumbers(1, 2, 3, 4, 5); // Outputs: [1, 2, 3, 4, 5]
```

In this example, the "printNumbers" function takes an indefinite number of numbers and stores them in an array of type "number".

Conclusion

Rest parameters are a useful feature in Typescript that allow you to represent an indefinite number of arguments as an array. They can be used to pass a variable number of arguments to another function or to perform calculations on a set of arguments. By using rest parameters and the spread operator, you can write flexible and reusable functions in Typescript.

Exercises

To review these concepts, we will go through a series of exercises designed to test your understanding and apply what you have learned.

Write a function named "concatStrings" that takes an indefinite number of strings and returns a single concatenated string.

Write a function named "findMax" that takes an indefinite number of numbers and returns the maximum number.

Write a function named "calculateTotal" that takes an indefinite number of numbers and returns their total sum.

Write a function named "countWords" that takes an indefinite number of strings and returns the total number of words.

Write a function named "flattenArray" that takes an indefinite number of arrays and returns a single flattened array.

Solutions

Write a function named "concatStrings" that takes an indefinite number of strings and returns a single concatenated string.

```
function concatStrings(...strings: string[]): string {
  return strings.join(' ');
}
console.log(concatStrings('Hello', 'world')); // Outputs: "Hello world"
console.log(concatStrings('Hello', 'world', '!')); // Outputs: "Hello world!"
```

Write a function named "findMax" that takes an indefinite number of numbers and returns the maximum number.

```typescript
function findMax(...numbers: number[]): number {
  return Math.max(...numbers);
}
console.log(findMax(1, 2, 3)); // Outputs: 3
console.log(findMax(5, 2, 10, 7, 3)); // Outputs: 10
console.log(findMax(-1, -5, -10)); // Outputs: -1
```

Write a function named "calculateTotal" that takes an indefinite number of numbers and returns their total sum.

```typescript
function calculateTotal(...numbers: number[]): number {
  let total = 0;
  for (const number of numbers) {
    total += number;
  }
  return total;
}
console.log(calculateTotal(1, 2, 3)); // Outputs: 6
console.log(calculateTotal(5, 2, 10, 7, 3)); // Outputs: 27
console.log(calculateTotal(-1, -5, -10)); // Outputs: -16
```

Write a function named "countWords" that takes an indefinite number of strings and returns the total number of words.

```typescript
function countWords(...strings: string[]): number {
  let total = 0;
  for (const string of strings) {
    total += string.split(' ').length;
  }
  return total;
}
console.log(countWords('Hello', 'world')); // Outputs: 2
console.log(countWords('The', 'quick', 'brown', 'fox', 'jumps', 'over', 'the', 'lazy', 'dog')); // Outputs: 9
console.log(countWords('This', 'is', 'a', 'sentence', 'with', 'five', 'words')); // Outputs: 7
```

Write a function named "flattenArray" that takes an indefinite number of arrays and returns a single flattened array.

```typescript
function flattenArray(...arrays: any[][]): any[] {
  return arrays.flat();
}
```

```
console.log(flattenArray([1, 2, 3], [4, 5, 6], [7, 8, 9])); // Outputs: [1, 2, 3, 4, 5, 6, 7, 8, 9]
console.log(flattenArray(['a', 'b', 'c'], ['d', 'e', 'f'], ['g', 'h', 'i'])); // Outputs: ['a', 'b', 'c', 'd', 'e', 'f', 'g', 'h', 'i']
console.log(flattenArray([true, false, true], [false, true, false])); // Outputs: [true, false, true, false, true, false]
```

UNDERSTANDING GENERICS AND WHY THEY ARE USEFUL

In this article, we will be exploring generics in Typescript. Generics allow you to create reusable code that can work with a variety of types, rather than being specific to just one type. This can be especially useful when working with functions and classes that need to operate on a variety of data types.

What are Generics?

Generics are a way to write code that can work with a variety of types, rather than being specific to just one type. They allow you to create code that is more flexible and reusable.

For example, consider a function that takes an array of numbers and returns the maximum value. Without generics, you would have to write a separate function for each data type: one for numbers, one for strings, etc. With generics, you can write a single function that works with any data type:

```typescript
function findMax<T>(arr: T[]): T {
  let max = arr[0];
  for (const item of arr) {
    if (item > max) {
      max = item;
    }
  }
  return max;
}
console.log(findMax([1, 2, 3])); // Outputs: 3
console.log(findMax(['a', 'b', 'c'])); // Outputs: 'c'
```

In the example above, we have defined a generic function named "findMax" that takes an array of type T and returns a value of type T. The "T" in angle brackets represents the generic type. When we call the function, we specify the type of "T" as a type argument.

Why are Generics Useful?

Generics are useful because they allow you to write code that is flexible and reusable. Instead of having to write separate functions for each data type, you can write a single function that can work with any data type. This can save you a lot of time and make your code easier to maintain.

Generics are also useful because they allow you to write code that is more type-safe. By specifying the type of "T" as a type argument, you can ensure that your function only operates on values of the correct type. This can help prevent type errors and make your code more reliable.

Using Generics with Classes

Generics can also be used with classes in Typescript. For example, consider a simple class that represents a stack:

```typescript
class Stack<T> {
  private items: T[] = [];
  push(item: T) {
    this.items.push(item);
  }
  pop(): T {
    return this.items.pop();
  }
}
const numberStack = new Stack<number>();
numberStack.push(1);
numberStack.push(2);
console.log(numberStack.pop()); // Outputs: 2
const stringStack = new Stack<string>();
stringStack.push('a');
stringStack.push('b');
console.log(stringStack.pop()); // Outputs: 'b'
```

In the example above, we have defined a class named "Stack" that takes a generic type "T". The "T" represents the type of the items in the stack. When we create a new instance of the class, we specify the type of "T" as a type argument. This allows us to create stacks of different data types: one for numbers and one for strings.

Conclusion

Generics are a powerful tool in Typescript that allow you to write flexible and reusable code. They can be used with functions and classes to create code that can work with a variety of data types. By specifying the generic type as a type argument, you can ensure that your code is type-safe and operates on the correct data types.

Using generics can save you a lot of time and make your code easier to maintain. They are an important concept to understand when working with Typescript and are useful in a variety of situations.

Exercises

To review these concepts, we will go through a series of exercises designed to test your understanding and apply what you have learned.

Write a generic function named "swap" that takes two parameters, "a" and "b", and swaps their values.

Write a generic function named "reverse" that takes an array and reverses the order of its elements.

Write a generic function named "removeItem" that takes an array and an item, and removes all occurrences of the item from the array.

Write a generic function named "groupBy" that takes an array and a key selector function, and returns an object where the keys are the selected values and the values are arrays of the corresponding elements.

Write a generic function named "unique" that takes an array and returns a new array with duplicate elements removed.

Solutions

Write a generic function named "swap" that takes two parameters, "a" and "b", and swaps their values.

```typescript
function swap<T>(a: T, b: T): void {
  const temp = a;
  a = b;
  b = temp;
}
let x = 1;
let y = 2;
swap(x, y);
console.log(x, y); // Outputs: 2, 1
let a = 'hello';
let b = 'world';
swap(a, b);
console.log(a, b); // Outputs: 'world', 'hello'
```

Write a generic function named "reverse" that takes an array and reverses the order of its elements.

```typescript
function reverse<T>(arr: T[]): T[] {
  return arr.reverse();
}
console.log(reverse([1, 2, 3])); // Outputs: [3, 2, 1]
console.log(reverse(['a', 'b', 'c'])); // Outputs: ['c', 'b', 'a']
```

```typescript
console.log(reverse([true, false, true])); // Outputs: [true, false, true]
```

Write a generic function named "removeItem" that takes an array and an item, and removes all occurrences of the item from the array.

```typescript
function removeItem<T>(arr: T[], item: T): T[] {
  return arr.filter(x => x !== item);
}
console.log(removeItem([1, 2, 3, 1, 2, 3], 1)); // Outputs: [2, 3, 2, 3]
console.log(removeItem(['a', 'b', 'c', 'a', 'b', 'c'], 'a')); // Outputs: ['b', 'c', 'b', 'c']
console.log(removeItem([true, false, true, false], true)); // Outputs: [false, false]
```

Write a generic function named "groupBy" that takes an array and a key selector function, and returns an object where the keys are the selected values and the values are arrays of the corresponding elements.

```typescript
function groupBy<T, K>(arr: T[], keySelector: (item: T) => K): Record<K, T[]> {
  const groups: Record<K, T[]> = {};
  for (const item of arr) {
   const key = keySelector(item);
   if (key in groups) {
    groups[key].push(item);
   } else {
    groups[key] = [item];
   }
  }
  return groups;
}
console.log(groupBy([1, 2, 3, 4, 5], x => x % 2 === 0));
// Outputs: { 'false': [1, 3, 5], 'true': [2, 4] }
```

Write a generic function named "unique" that takes an array and returns a new array with duplicate elements removed.

```typescript
function unique<T>(arr: T[]): T[] {
  return Array.from(new Set(arr));
}
console.log(unique([1, 2, 3, 2, 1])); // Outputs: [1, 2, 3]
console.log(unique(['a', 'b', 'c', 'b', 'a'])); // Outputs: ['a', 'b', 'c']
console.log(unique([true, false, true, false])); // Outputs: [true, false]
```

DECLARING AND USING GENERICS IN FUNCTIONS, CLASSES, AND INTERFACES

Generics are a powerful feature in TypeScript that allow you to create reusable components that can work with a variety of types. They are particularly useful when you need to write functions, classes, or interfaces that can work with multiple types, but you don't want to have to write separate versions for each type.

In this article, we'll look at how to declare and use generics in functions, classes, and interfaces in TypeScript.

Declaring Generics in Functions

To declare a generic in a function, you use the angle brackets <> and give the generic a name. For example:

```
function identity<T>(arg: T): T {
  return arg;
}
```

In this example, the function "identity" takes an argument of type T and returns a value of type T. The type T is a generic type parameter, and it can be any type.

To call the function, you can specify the type parameter by using the type in angle brackets:

```
let output = identity<string>('Hello');
// output: string
```

You can also leave out the type parameter and let TypeScript infer the type from the argument:

```
let output = identity('Hello');
// output: string
```

Declaring Generics in Classes

To declare a generic in a class, you use the same syntax as in a function. For example:

```
class GenericNumber<T> {
  zeroValue: T;
```

```
add: (x: T, y: T) => T;
}
let myGenericNumber = new GenericNumber<number>();
myGenericNumber.zeroValue = 0;
myGenericNumber.add = function(x, y) { return x + y; };
```

In this example, the class "GenericNumber" has a generic type parameter T, which is used for the "zeroValue" and "add" properties.

Declaring Generics in Interfaces

To declare a generic in an interface, you use the same syntax as in a function or class. For example:

```
interface GenericIdentityFn {
 <T>(arg: T): T;
}
let myIdentity: GenericIdentityFn = function<T>(arg: T): T {
 return arg;
}
```

In this example, the interface "GenericIdentityFn" has a generic type parameter T, which is used for the argument and return type of the function.

Using Generics with Type Constraints

Sometimes you may want to specify a constraint on the types that can be used as the generic type parameter. To do this, you can use the "extends" keyword followed by a type.

For example, you may want to create a function that works with arrays, but only arrays of a certain type. You can do this by adding a type constraint to the generic type parameter:

```
function copyArray<T extends number | string>(arr: T[]): T[] {
 return arr.slice();
}
let numArr = [1, 2, 3];
let strArr = ['a', 'b', 'c'];
let numArrCopy = copyArray(numArr); // numArrCopy: number[]
let strArrCopy = copyArray(strArr); // strArrCopy: string[]
```

Using Generics with Class Types

You can also use generics with class types. For example, you can create a generic "Factory" class that creates instances of a specific class. To do this, you can use the "new" keyword and the "Class" type:

```
class Factory<T> {
```

```
create(c: {new(): T;}): T {
  return new c();
}
}
class Product {
  name: string;
}
let factory = new Factory<Product>();
let product = factory.create(Product);
product.name = 'Product 1';
```

In this example, the "Factory" class has a generic type parameter T, which is used to specify the type of the "create" method's return value. The "create" method takes a class constructor as its argument, and it returns an instance of the class.

Conclusion

Generics are a powerful feature in TypeScript that allow you to create reusable components that can work with a variety of types. They are particularly useful when you need to write functions, classes, or interfaces that can work with multiple types, but you don't want to have to write separate versions for each type.

In this article, we looked at how to declare and use generics in functions, classes, and interfaces in TypeScript. We also looked at how to use generics with type constraints and class types.

With this knowledge, you should be able to use generics effectively in your TypeScript projects to create more flexible and reusable code.

Exercises

To review these concepts, we will go through a series of exercises designed to test your understanding and apply what you have learned.

Write a generic function named "swap" that takes two variables and swaps their values.

Write a generic function named "findIndex" that takes an array and a value, and returns the index of the value in the array if it exists, or -1 if it does not.

Write a generic class named "SortedArray" that implements a sorted array data structure. The sorted array should have the following methods: "add", "remove", and "search". The array should always be sorted in ascending order.

Write a function named "unique" that takes in an array of values and returns an array with only the unique values. Use generics to make the function work with any type of value.

Write a function named "groupBy" that takes in an array of values and a key extractor function, and returns an object with keys for each unique value returned by the key extractor function. Use generics to make the function work with any type of value.

Solutions

Write a generic function named "swap" that takes two variables and swaps their values.

```
function swap<T>(a: T, b: T): [T, T] {
 return [b, a];
}
let a = 1;
let b = 'b';
let c = true;
console.log(swap(a, b)); // Output: ['b', 1]
console.log(swap(b, c)); // Output: [true, 'b']
console.log(swap(a, c)); // Output: [true, 1]
```

Write a generic function named "findIndex" that takes an array and a value, and returns the index of the value in the array if it exists, or -1 if it does not.

```
function findIndex<T>(arr: T[], value: T): number {
 return arr.indexOf(value);
}
console.log(findIndex([1, 2, 3, 4, 5], 3)); // Output: 2
console.log(findIndex(['a', 'b', 'c', 'd'], 'b')); // Output: 1
console.log(findIndex([true, false, true], false)); // Output: 1
console.log(findIndex([1, 2, 3, 4, 5], 6)); // Output: -1
```

Write a generic class named "SortedArray" that implements a sorted array data structure. The sorted array should have the following methods: "add", "remove", and "search". The array should always be sorted in ascending order.

```
class SortedArray<T> {
 private arr: T[] = [];
 add(value: T) {
  this.arr.push(value);
  this.arr.sort();
 }
 remove(value: T) {
  let index = this.arr.indexOf(value);
  if (index >= 0) {
   this.arr.splice(index, 1);
   return true;
  }
```

```
    return false;
  }
  search(value: T) {
    return this.arr.includes(value);
  }
}
let sortedArray = new SortedArray<number>();
sortedArray.add(5);
sortedArray.add(2);
sortedArray.add(1);
sortedArray.add(3);
console.log(sortedArray.search(1)); // Output: true
console.log(sortedArray.search(4)); // Output: false
console.log(sortedArray.remove(1)); // Output: true
console.log(sortedArray.remove(4)); // Output: false
```

Write a function named "unique" that takes in an array of values and returns an array with only the unique values. Use generics to make the function work with any type of value.

```
function unique<T>(arr: T[]): T[] {
  return [...new Set(arr)];
}
console.log(unique([1, 2, 3, 3, 4, 4, 4, 5, 5])); // Output: [1, 2, 3, 4, 5]
console.log(unique(['a', 'a', 'b', 'b', 'c', 'c'])) // Output: ['a', 'b', 'c']
```

Write a function named "groupBy" that takes in an array of values and a key extractor function, and returns an object with keys for each unique value returned by the key extractor function. Use generics to make the function work with any type of value.

```
function groupBy<T, K>(arr: T[], keyExtractor: (item: T) => K): {[key: K]: T[]} {
  let groups: {[key: K]: T[]} = {};
  for (let item of arr) {
    let key = keyExtractor(item);
    if (!groups[key]) {
      groups[key] = [];
    }
    groups[key].push(item);
  }
  return groups;
}
```

```
console.log(groupBy([1, 2, 3, 3, 4, 4, 4, 5, 5], (x) => x % 2 === 0));
// Output: { 'true': [ 2, 4, 4, 4 ], 'false': [ 1, 3, 3, 5, 5 ] }
console.log(groupBy(['a', 'a', 'b', 'b', 'c', 'c'], (x) => x))
// Output: { a: [ 'a', 'a' ], b: [ 'b', 'b' ], c: [ 'c', 'c' ] }
```

CONSTRAINING GENERICS WITH TYPE PARAMETERS

In Typescript, it is possible to constrain the types that can be used as arguments for a generic function or class by using type parameters. This can be useful when you want to ensure that a function or class only works with certain types of values, or when you want to access properties or methods of those values that are specific to a certain type. In this article, we will look at how to use type parameters to constrain generics and how to use them effectively in your code.

What are Type Parameters?

Type parameters are special placeholders that you can use in the definition of a generic function or class to specify the types of the arguments or properties that the function or class can take. For example, if you have a generic function that takes an argument of type T, you can specify that T must be a number by using the syntax function myFunction<T extends number>(arg: T). This means that the myFunction function can only be called with an argument of type number, and the type of the arg parameter will be inferred as number.

Type parameters can also be used to specify that a function or class can only work with certain types of values. For example, you might want to create a generic function that only works with arrays of a certain type. In this case, you can specify a type parameter for the array element type, like this: function myFunction<T>(arr: T[]). This specifies that the myFunction function can only be called with an array of values of type T.

Type parameters are very useful for creating flexible and reusable code, but they can also make your code more difficult to read and understand if they are not used correctly. It is important to use type parameters appropriately and only when they are necessary, to ensure that your code is easy to understand and maintain.

Using Type Parameters to Constrain Generics

One of the main benefits of using type parameters is that you can use them to constrain the types that a generic function or class can take. For example, you might want to create a generic function that only works with arrays of numbers, or a class that only works with objects that have a certain property.

To constrain a type parameter, you can use the extends keyword followed by the type that you want to constrain the parameter to. For example, to specify that a type parameter T must be a number, you can use the following syntax: function myFunction<T extends number>(arg: T). This specifies that the myFunction function can only be called with an argument of type number, and the type of the argparameter will be inferred as number.

You can also use the extends keyword to specify that a type parameter must be a subclass of a certain class or implement a certain interface. For example, to specify that a type parameter T must be a subclass of the Person class, you can use the following syntax: function myFunction<T extends Person>(arg: T). This specifies that the myFunction function can only be called with an argument of type Person or a subclass of Person, and the type of the arg parameter will be inferred as the subclass type.

Using Type Parameters in Function Arguments and Return Types

Type parameters can be used in the arguments and return types of a generic function to specify the types of the values that the function can take and return. For example, you might want to create a generic function that takes an argument of type T and returns a value of type U. In this case, you can specify the type parameters T and U in the function definition, like this: function myFunction<T, U>(arg: T): U. This specifies that the myFunction function can be called with an argument of any type, and it will return a value of any type.

You can also use type parameters to specify that a function can only take certain types of arguments or return certain types of values. For example, you might want to create a generic function that takes an argument of type T and returns a value of type T. In this case, you can specify the same type parameter for both the argument and the return type, like this: function myFunction<T>(arg: T): T. This specifies that the myFunction function can only be called with an argument of the same type as the return value, and the type of both the argument and the return value will be inferred from the type of the argument.

Using Type Parameters in Class Properties and Methods

Type parameters can also be used in the properties and methods of a generic class to specify the types of the values that the class can hold and manipulate. For example, you might want to create a generic class that has a property of type T and a method that takes an argument of type U. In this case, you can specify the type parameters T and U in the class definition, like this:

```
class MyClass<T, U> {
property: T;
method(arg: U): void {
  // code here
}
}
```

This specifies that the MyClass class has a property of any type and a method that can be called with an argument of any type. You can use the same type parameter for both the property and the method, or you can use different type parameters for each.

Using Type Parameters Effectively

When using type parameters in your code, it is important to use them appropriately and only when they are necessary. Type parameters can make your code more flexible and reusable, but they can also make your code more difficult to read and understand if they are not used correctly.

Here are a few tips for using type parameters effectively:

- Use type parameters to specify the types of the arguments and return values of a generic function or the properties and methods of a generic class.
- Use the extends keyword to constrain type parameters to certain types or subclasses.
- Use the same type parameter for related values, such as the argument and return value of a function or the property and method of a class.
- Don't use type parameters unnecessarily. If a function or class doesn't need to be generic, don't use type parameters.
- Use descriptive names for type parameters to make your code easier to read and understand.

Conclusion

Type parameters are a powerful tool in Typescript for creating flexible and reusable code. By using type parameters to constrain the types that a generic function or class can take, you can create code that is easy to understand and maintain. Remember to use type parameters appropriately and only when they are necessary, and your code will be easier to read and understand.

Exercises

To review these concepts, we will go through a series of exercises designed to test your understanding and apply what you have learned.

Create a generic function mapArray that takes in an array of elements of type T and a function f that takes an element of type T and returns an element of type U. The mapArray function should return a new array of elements of type U that are the result of calling the function f on each element of the input array.

Create a generic class Pair that has two properties, first and second, both of type T. The Pair class should have a method swap that swaps the values of the first and second properties.

Create a generic function filterArray that takes in an array of elements of type T and a function predicate that takes an element of type T and returns a boolean. The filterArray function should return a new array of elements of type T that are the elements of the input array for which the predicate function returns true.

Create a generic class Queue that has a property items of type T[]. The Queue class should have the following methods:
(1) enqueue: takes an element of type T and adds it to the end of the items array. (2) dequeue: removes and returns the element at the front of the items array.

Create a generic class Stack that has a property items of type T[]. The Stack class should have the following methods: (1) push: takes an element of type T and adds it to the top of the items (2) pop: removes and returns the element at the top of the items array.

Solutions

Create a generic function mapArray that takes in an array of elements of type T and a function f that takes an element of type T and returns an element of type U. The mapArray function should return a new array of elements of type U that are the result of calling the function f on each element of the input array.

```
function mapArray<T, U>(array: T[], f: (x: T) => U): U[] {
let result: U[] = [];
for (let i = 0; i < array.length; i++) {
  result.push(f(array[i]));
}
return result;
}
```

Create a generic class Pair that has two properties, first and second, both of type T. The Pair class should have a method swap that swaps the values of the first and second properties.

```
class Pair<T> {
first: T;
second: T;
constructor(first: T, second: T) {
  this.first = first;
  this.second = second;
}
swap(): void {
  let temp = this.first;
  this.first = this.second;
  this.second = temp;
}
}
```

Create a generic function filterArray that takes in an array of elements of type T and a function predicate that takes an element of type T and returns a boolean. The filterArray function should return a new array of elements of type T that are the elements of the input array for which the predicate function returns true.

```
function filterArray<T>(array: T[], predicate: (x: T) => boolean): T[] {
let result: T[] = [];
for (let i = 0; i < array.length; i++) {
  if (predicate(array[i])) {
    result.push(array[i]);
  }
```

```
}
    return result;
}
```

Create a generic class Queue **that has a property** items **of type** T[]. **The** Queue **class should have the following methods:**

(1) enqueue: **takes an element of type** T **and adds it to the end of the** items **array. (2)** dequeue: **removes and returns the element at the front of the** items **array.**

```
class Queue<T> {
  items: T[];
  constructor() {
    this.items = [];
  }
  enqueue(item: T): void {
    this.items.push(item);
  }
  dequeue(): T | undefined {
    return this.items.shift();
  }
}
```

Create a generic class Stack **that has a property** items **of type** T[]. **The** Stack **class should have the following methods: (1)** push: **takes an element of type** T **and adds it to the top of the** items **(2)** pop: **removes and returns the element at the top of the** items **array.**

```
class Stack<T> {
  items: T[];
  constructor() {
    this.items = [];
  }
  push(item: T): void {
    this.items.push(item);
  }
  pop(): T | undefined {
    return this.items.pop();
  }
}
```

ENUMS IN TYPESCRIPT

Enums, short for enumerations, are a feature in Typescript that allow you to define a set of named constants. Enums are a powerful tool that can be used to improve the readability and maintainability of your code. In this article, we will explore the basics of enums in Typescript and learn how to use them effectively in our projects.

What are Enums?

Enums are a way to define a set of named constants in Typescript. They are a kind of data type that consists of a set of named values, called members. Each member has a name and a value associated with it. The value of an enum member can be a string or a number, and it is usually an integer.

Here's an example of an enum in Typescript:

```
enum Days {
  Sunday,
  Monday,
  Tuesday,
  Wednesday,
  Thursday,
  Friday,
  Saturday
}
```

In this example, we have defined an enum called Days with seven members, each representing a day of the week. By default, the value of each member is its position in the enum, starting at 0 for the first member. So, in this example, Sunday has a value of 0, Monday has a value of 1, and so on.

You can also specify the value of an enum member explicitly, like this:

```
enum Days {
  Sunday = 1,
  Monday,
  Tuesday,
  Wednesday,
  Thursday,
  Friday,
```

```
Saturday
}
```

In this case, Sunday has a value of 1, Monday has a value of 2, and so on. You can also use strings as the value of an enum member, like this:

```
enum Days {
  Sunday = "SUN",
  Monday = "MON",
  Tuesday = "TUE",
  Wednesday = "WED",
  Thursday = "THU",
  Friday = "FRI",
  Saturday = "SAT"
}
```

In this example, each member has a string value representing the abbreviation of the day of the week.

Using Enums:

Once you have defined an enum, you can use its members in your code just like any other variable. For example, you can use an enum member as a value for a function parameter or as the return type of a function.

```
function getDayName(day: Days): string {
  switch (day) {
    case Days.Sunday:
      return "Sunday";
    case Days.Monday:
      return "Monday";
    // ...
  }
}
```

In this example, we have defined a function called getDayName that takes a Days enum member as a parameter and returns a string with the name of the day of the week.

You can also use the enum keyword to get the value of an enum member. For example:

```
console.log(Days.Sunday); // outputs 0
console.log(Days[0]); // outputs "Sunday"
```

In the first line, we are logging the value of the Sunday member, which is 0. In the second line, we are logging the name of the member with a value of 0, which is "Sunday".

Advantages of Enums:

Enums, or enumerations, are a powerful feature in Typescript that allow developers to define a set of named constants. This can be especially useful when working with a fixed set of values that are meant to be represented as a group, such as the days of the week or the suits in a deck of cards.

One of the main advantages of using enums is that they provide a clear and concise way to represent a group of related values. This can help to improve the readability and maintainability of your code, as it clearly defines the values that are expected and allows you to easily reference them throughout your codebase.

Another advantage of enums is that they allow you to assign a specific type to each member, which can be especially useful when working with large codebases where it may not always be clear what type a particular value should be. By using enums, you can ensure that all members are of the same type and that the type is clearly defined and easy to understand.

Finally, enums can also help to improve the performance of your code by allowing the Typescript compiler to optimize the code for the specific values that are being used. This can result in faster and more efficient code, which can be especially important when working with large and complex projects.

Overall, enums are a valuable tool for developers working with Typescript, and can help to improve the readability, maintainability, and performance of your code.

Advanced Features of Enums:

Enums also have some advanced features that you can use to customize their behavior and make them even more useful.

One of these features is the ability to define computed members in an enum. Computed members are members whose value is computed at runtime based on an expression. For example:

```
enum Days {
Sunday,
Monday,
Tuesday,
Wednesday,
Thursday,
Friday,
Saturday,
Total = Sunday + Saturday + 1
}
```

In this example, the Total member is a computed member that is calculated at runtime based on the values of the Sunday and Saturday members. The result of this expression is 7, which is the total number of days in a week.

Another advanced feature of enums is the ability to define constant members. Constant members are members whose value cannot be changed after the enum is defined. For example:

```
enum Days {
Sunday,
Monday,
Tuesday,
Wednesday,
Thursday,
Friday,
Saturday,
Total = Sunday + Saturday + 1,
readonly Weekend = Sunday + Saturday
}
```

In this example, the Weekend member is a constant member whose value is the sum of the values of the Sunday and Saturday members. This value cannot be changed after the enum is defined.

Conclusion

Enums are a useful feature in Typescript that can help you improve the readability and maintainability of your code. They allow you to define a set of named constants and use them in your code just like any other variable. With advanced features like computed members and constant members, enums can be customized to fit your specific needs.

Exercises

To review these concepts, we will go through a series of exercises designed to test your understanding and apply what you have learned.

Write a function called getDayNumber that takes a day name (a string) as a parameter and returns the corresponding day number from the Days enum. If the day name is not a valid member of the enum, the function should return -1.

Write a function called isWeekend that takes a day number (a number) as a parameter and returns a boolean indicating whether the day is a weekend day or not. You should use the Days enum to determine the weekend days.

Write a function called getDayNameFromNumber that takes a day number (a number) as a parameter and returns the corresponding day name from the Days enum. If the day number is not a valid member of the enum, the function should return null.

Write a function called getNextWeekday that takes a day name (a string) as a parameter and returns the name of the next weekday. For example, if the input is "Monday", the output should be "Tuesday". If the input is "Friday", the output should be "Monday". You should use the Days enum to determine the next weekday.

Write a function called isWeekday that takes a day name (a string) as a parameter and returns a boolean indicating whether the day is a weekday or not. You should use the Days enum to determine the weekdays.

Solutions

Write a function called getDayNumber **that takes a day name (a string) as a parameter and returns the corresponding day number from the** Days **enum. If the day name is not a valid member of the enum, the function should return** -1.

```
function getDayNumber(dayName: string): number {
  switch (dayName) {
    case "Sunday":
      return Days.Sunday;
    case "Monday":
      return Days.Monday;
    case "Tuesday":
      return Days.Tuesday;
    case "Wednesday":
      return Days.Wednesday;
    case "Thursday":
      return Days.Thursday;
    case "Friday":
      return Days.Friday;
    case "Saturday":
      return Days.Saturday;
    default:
      return -1;
  }
}
```

Write a function called isWeekend **that takes a day number (a number) as a parameter and returns a boolean indicating whether the day is a weekend day or not. You should use the** Days **enum to determine the weekend days.**

```
function isWeekend(dayNumber: number): boolean {
  return dayNumber === Days.Sunday || dayNumber === Days.Saturday;
}
```

Write a function called getDayNameFromNumber **that takes a day number (a number) as a parameter and returns the corresponding day name from the** Days **enum. If the day number is not a valid member of the enum, the function should return** null.

```
function getDayNameFromNumber(dayNumber: number): string | null {
  switch (dayNumber) {
```

```
case Days.Sunday:
    return "Sunday";
case Days.Monday:
    return "Monday";
case Days.Tuesday:
    return "Tuesday";
case Days.Wednesday:
    return "Wednesday";
case Days.Thursday:
    return "Thursday";
case Days.Friday:
    return "Friday";
case Days.Saturday:
    return "Saturday";
default:
    return null;
    }
}
```

Write a function called getNextWeekday that takes a day name (a string) as a parameter and returns the name of the next weekday. For example, if the input is "Monday", the output should be "Tuesday". If the input is "Friday", the output should be "Monday". You should use the Days enum to determine the next weekday.

```
function getPreviousWeekday(dayName: string): string {
    const dayNumber = getDayNumber(dayName);
    if (dayNumber === Days.Monday) {
        return "Friday";
    } else {
        return getDayNameFromNumber(dayNumber - 1);
    }
}
```

Write a function called isWeekday that takes a day name (a string) as a parameter and returns a boolean indicating whether the day is a weekday or not. You should use the Days enum to determine the weekdays.

```
function isWeekday(dayName: string): boolean {
    const dayNumber = getDayNumber(dayName);
    return dayNumber > Days.Sunday && dayNumber < Days.Saturday;
```

DECORATORS IN TYPESCRIPT

Decorators are a powerful feature in Typescript that allow you to modify the behavior of a class, method, or property at runtime. In this article, we will explore the basics of decorators and how they work in Typescript.

What are Decorators?

Decorators are functions that are used to add additional behavior to a class, method, or property. They are called "decorators" because they decorate or modify the target class, method, or property with additional functionality.

Decorators are implemented as functions, and they take the target class, method, or property as their first parameter. For example, here is the syntax for a class decorator:

```
function myDecorator(target: Function) {
    // Decorator logic goes here
}
```

And here is the syntax for a method decorator:

```
function myDecorator(target: Object, propertyKey: string, descriptor: PropertyDescriptor) {
    // Decorator logic goes here
}
```

And here is the syntax for a property decorator:

```
function myDecorator(target: Object, propertyKey: string) {
    // Decorator logic goes here
}
```

How to Use Decorators in Typescript

To use a decorator in Typescript, you simply need to add the decorator function to the class, method, or property that you want to decorate. For example, here is how you would use a class decorator:

```
@myDecorator
class MyClass {
    // Class logic goes here
}
```

And here is how you would use a method decorator:

```
class MyClass {
@myDecorator
myMethod() {
  // Method logic goes here
}
}
```

And here is how you would use a property decorator:

```
class MyClass {
@myDecorator
myProperty: string;
}
```

Decorator Example: Logging Method Calls

To demonstrate how decorators work in Typescript, let's look at an example of a decorator that logs the name and arguments of a method every time it is called.

Here is how you could define the logMethod decorator:

```
function logMethod(target: Object, propertyKey: string, descriptor: PropertyDescriptor) {
  const originalMethod = descriptor.value;
  descriptor.value = function(...args: any[]) {
   console.log(`Calling method ${propertyKey} with args: ${args}`);
   return originalMethod.apply(this, args);
  }
}
```

This decorator function takes three arguments:

- target: The prototype of the class that the decorated method belongs to.
- propertyKey: The name of the decorated method.
- descriptor: The property descriptor of the decorated method.

The decorator function first stores the original method in a variable, and then replaces it with a new function that logs the method name and arguments before calling the original method.

To use this decorator, you would apply it to a method like this:

```
class MyClass {
@logMethod
myMethod(arg1: string, arg2: number) {
  console.log(`Inside myMethod with args: ${arg1}, ${arg2}`);
```

```
  }
}
```

Now, every time you call myMethod, it will log the name and arguments of the method:

```
const myClass = new MyClass();
myClass.myMethod('hello', 123);
// Output: "Calling method myMethod with args: hello, 123"
```

You can also use decorators with getters and setters in the same way:

```
class MyClass {
  private _myProp: string;
  @logMethod
  get myProp() {
    return this._myProp;
  }
  @logMethod
  set myProp(value: string) {
    this._myProp = value;
  }
}
const myClass = new MyClass();
myClass.myProp = 'hello';
console.log(myClass.myProp);
// Output: "Calling method get myProp with args: "
// Output: "Calling method set myProp with args: hello"
```

Note that the decorator function is called with the get or set keyword, depending on which accessor is being decorated.In this example, we saw how to use a decorator to log the name and arguments of a method every time it is called.

Decorator Factories

In addition to standalone decorators, Typescript also allows you to create decorator factories. A decorator factory is a function that returns a decorator function. This can be useful when you want to pass parameters to your decorator.

For example, here is how you could create a decorator factory that logs the name of a method along with the time it takes to execute:

```
function timeMethod(logMessage: string) {
  return function(target: Object, propertyKey: string, descriptor: PropertyDescriptor) {
```

```
const originalMethod = descriptor.value;
descriptor.value = function(...args: any[]) {
  console.time(logMessage);
  const result = originalMethod.apply(this, args);
  console.timeEnd(logMessage);
  return result;
  }
 }
}
```

To use this decorator factory, you would call it with the desired log message as its argument:

```
class MyClass {
@timeMethod('MyMethod')
myMethod(arg1: string, arg2: number) {
  console.log(`Inside myMethod with args: ${arg1}, ${arg2}`);
 }
}
```

This will log the time it takes to execute myMethod along with the message "MyMethod".

Decorator Composition

In addition to standalone decorators and decorator factories, Typescript also allows you to compose decorators by applying multiple decorators to a single class, method, or property.

For example, you could apply both the logMethod and timeMethod decorators to the myMethod method like this:

```
class MyClass {
@logMethod
@timeMethod('MyMethod')
myMethod(arg1: string, arg2: number) {
  console.log(`Inside myMethod with args: ${arg1}, ${arg2}`);
 }
}
```

This would log the time it takes to execute myMethod along with a message, as well as log a message every time myMethod is called.

Conclusion

Decorators are a powerful feature in Typescript that allow you to modify the behavior of a class, method, or property at runtime. They can be used to add additional functionality to your code, and they are easy to use and compose. In this article, we covered the basics of decorators and how they work in Typescript.

Exercises

To review these concepts, we will go through a series of exercises designed to test your understanding and apply what you have learned.

Create a decorator function called logProperty **that logs the value of a property every time it is accessed or modified.**
Create a decorator function called readonly **that makes a property read-only, meaning it can only be accessed and not modified.**
Create a decorator function called memoize **that caches the results of a function and returns the cached value if the function is called with the same arguments.**
Create a decorator function called throttle **that limits the number of times a function can be called within a given time interval.**
Create a decorator factory function called logCalls **that logs the arguments and return value of a function every time it is called.**

Solutions

Create a decorator function called logProperty **that logs the value of a property every time it is accessed or modified.**

Here is an example of how you could use the decorator:

```
class MyClass {
  @logProperty
  myProp: string;
}
const myClass = new MyClass();
myClass.myProp = 'hello';
console.log(myClass.myProp);
```

Output:

```
Setting property myProp to value: hello
Getting property myProp with value: hello
```

Solution:

```
function logProperty(target: Object, propertyKey: string) {
  let value: any;
  const getter = () => {
    console.log(`Getting property ${propertyKey} with value: ${value}`);
    return value;
```

```
};
const setter = (newValue: any) => {
  console.log(`Setting property ${propertyKey} to value: ${newValue}`);
  value = newValue;
};
Object.defineProperty(target, propertyKey, {
  get: getter,
  set: setter,
});
}
```

Create a decorator function called readonly **that makes a property read-only, meaning it can only be accessed and not modified.**

Here is an example of how you could use the decorator:

```
class MyClass {
  @readonly
  myProp: string;
}
const myClass = new MyClass();
myClass.myProp = 'hello'; // This should throw an error
console.log(myClass.myProp);
```

Output:

```
Cannot assign to read only property 'myProp'
```

Solution:

```
function readonly(target: Object, propertyKey: string) {
  Object.defineProperty(target, propertyKey, {
    writable: false,
  });
}
```

Create a decorator function called memoize **that caches the results of a function and returns the cached value if the function is called with the same arguments.**

Here is an example of how you could use the decorator:

```
class MyClass {
  @memoize()
  slowFunction(a: number, b: number) {
```

```
  console.log('This function is slow');
  return a + b;
 }
}
const myClass = new MyClass();
console.log(myClass.slowFunction(1, 2)); // This should log "This function is slow" and return 3
console.log(myClass.slowFunction(1, 2)); // This should not log anything and return 3
console.log(myClass.slowFunction(3, 4)); // This should log "This function is slow" and return 7
```

Output:

```
This function is slow
3
This function is slow
7
```

Solution:

```
function memoize() {
 return function(target: Object, propertyKey: string, descriptor: PropertyDescriptor) {
  const originalMethod = descriptor.value;
  const cache = new Map<string, any>();
  descriptor.value = function(...args: any[]) {
   const key = JSON.stringify(args);
   if (!cache.has(key)) {
    cache.set(key, originalMethod.apply(this, args));
   }
   return cache.get(key);
  };
 };
}
```

Create a decorator function called throttle **that limits the number of times a function can be called within a given time interval.**

Here is an example of how you could use the decorator:

```
class MyClass {
 @throttle(500)
 myMethod() {
  console.log('This method is called');
```

```
  }
}
const myClass = new MyClass();
myClass.myMethod(); // This should log "This method is called"
myClass.myMethod(); // This should not log anything
setTimeout(() => {
  myClass.myMethod(); // This should log "This method is called"
}, 600);
```

Output:

```
This method is called
This method is called
```

Solution:

```
function throttle(interval: number) {
  return function(target: Object, propertyKey: string, descriptor: PropertyDescriptor) {
    const originalMethod = descriptor.value;
    let lastCall = 0;
    descriptor.value = function(...args: any[]) {
      const currentTime = Date.now();
      if (currentTime - lastCall > interval) {
        lastCall = currentTime;
        return originalMethod.apply(this, args);
      }
    };
  };
}
```

Create a decorator factory function called logCalls **that logs the arguments and return value of a function every time it is called.**

Here is an example of how you could use the decorator:

```
class MyClass {
@logCalls()
myMethod(a: number, b: number) {
  return a + b;
}
}
```

```
const myClass = new MyClass();
console.log(myClass.myMethod(1, 2)); // This should log "myMethod called with arguments 1, 2 and returned 3"
console.log(myClass.myMethod(3, 4)); // This should log "myMethod called with arguments 3, 4 and returned 7"
```

Output:

```
myMethod called with arguments 1, 2 and returned 3
myMethod called with arguments 3, 4 and returned 7
```

Solution:

```
function logCalls() {
 return function(target: Object, propertyKey: string, descriptor: PropertyDescriptor) {
  const originalMethod = descriptor.value;
  descriptor.value = function(...args: any[]) {
      console.log(`${propertyKey} called with arguments ${args} and returned ${originalMethod.apply(this, args)}`);
  };
 };
}
```

NAMESPACES IN TYPESCRIPT

Namespaces are a way to organize your code in large projects, particularly when you want to avoid naming collisions between different parts of your codebase. In TypeScript, you can use namespaces to create a logical structure for your code, similar to how you might use modules in other programming languages.

In this article, we will cover how to declare and use namespaces in TypeScript, as well as how to combine namespaces with other language features such as classes and interfaces. By the end of this article, you will have a good understanding of how to use namespaces to organize your TypeScript code and avoid naming conflicts.

Declaring a Namespace:

To declare a namespace in TypeScript, you can use the namespace keyword followed by the name of your namespace. Here is an example of a simple namespace declaration:

```
namespace MyNamespace {
  // Code goes here
}
```

You can then use the namespace by prefixing the name of the namespace followed by a dot and the name of the item you want to access. For example, to access a variable inside the MyNamespace namespace, you would use the following syntax:

```
MyNamespace.myVariable;
```

You can also nest namespaces within each other to create a hierarchy of namespaces. Here is an example of how you might use nested namespaces:

```
namespace MyNamespace {
  export namespace InnerNamespace {
    export const myVariable = 'Hello';
  }
}
console.log(MyNamespace.InnerNamespace.myVariable); // Outputs "Hello"
```

Combining Namespaces with Other Language Features:

One of the key benefits of namespaces is that you can use them in combination with other language features such as classes and interfaces. For example, you can use a namespace to group together a set of related classes and interfaces, like this:

```
namespace MyNamespace {
export class MyClass {
  // Code goes here
}
export interface MyInterface {
  // Code goes here
}
}
```

You can then use these classes and interfaces by prefixing them with the namespace name, like this:

```
const myObject = new MyNamespace.MyClass();
```

Using the export keyword in combination with namespaces allows you to make the classes and interfaces available outside of the namespace, so they can be used by other parts of your codebase.

Merging Namespaces:

In some cases, you may want to split a namespace across multiple files in your project. To do this, you can use the namespace merging feature in TypeScript.

To merge two namespaces, you can use the same namespace name in both files, like this:

```
// File 1
namespace MyNamespace {
 export const myVariable = 'Hello';
}
// File 2
namespace MyNamespace {
 export function myFunction() {
   console.log(myVariable);
 }
}
// File 3
console.log(MyNamespace.myVariable); // Outputs "Hello"
MyNamespace.myFunction(); // Outputs "Hello"
```

In this example, the MyNamespace namespace is defined in both File 1 and File 2, and the two definitions are merged together when the code is compiled. This allows you to split up a namespace across multiple files while maintaining a clear and organized structure for your code.

Using the namespace merging feature in TypeScript can be very useful in large projects, as it allows you to split up your code into smaller, more manageable chunks. However, it's important to note that you should use namespace merging with caution, as it can lead to unexpected behavior if you're not careful.

For example, if you have two files that define the same namespace and both files contain a class or interface with the same name, the two definitions will be merged together. This can lead to confusing errors and bugs if you're not careful, as the merged definitions may not behave as you expect.

To avoid these issues, it's a good idea to use a consistent naming convention for your namespaces and avoid defining the same item multiple times within the same namespace.

Conclusion:

In this article, we covered the basics of namespaces in TypeScript, including how to declare and use namespaces, how to combine namespaces with other language features, and how to merge namespaces across multiple files. By following the best practices outlined in this article, you can use namespaces to organize your TypeScript code and avoid naming conflicts in large projects.

Exercises

To review these concepts, we will go through a series of exercises designed to test your understanding and apply what you have learned.

Create a namespace called MyMath **that contains a function called** calculateSum **that takes two numbers as arguments and returns their sum. Test the function by calling it and logging the result to the console.**

Create a namespace called Shape **that contains an interface called** IShape **with a single property called** area. **Create a class called** Rectangle **that implements the** IShape**interface and has a method called** calculateArea **that calculates and returns the area of the rectangle. Test the** Rectangle **class by creating an instance of it and calling the** calculateArea **method.**

Create a namespace called MyUtils **that contains a class called** DateUtils **with a static method called** getCurrentDate **that returns the current date. Create another namespace called** MyApp **that uses the** MyUtils **namespace and calls the** getCurrentDate **method to log the current date to the console.**

Create a namespace called Animal **that contains an interface called** IAnimal **with a single property called** name. **Create a second namespace called** Dog **that extends the** Animal **namespace and contains a class called** Dog **that implements the** IAnimal**interface. Create an instance of the** Dog **class and log its** name **property to the console.**

Create a namespace called MyMath **that contains a function called** calculateSum **that takes two numbers as arguments and returns their sum. Create a second namespace called** MyApp **that also contains a function called** calculateSum **that takes three numbers as arguments and returns their sum. Use the** namespace merging **feature to merge the** MyMath **namespace into the** MyApp **namespace and test the** calculateSum **function by calling it and logging the result to the console.**

Solutions

Create a namespace called MyMath that contains a function called calculateSum that takes two numbers as arguments and returns their sum. Test the function by calling it and logging the result to the console.

```typescript
namespace MyMath {
  export function calculateSum(num1: number, num2: number) {
    return num1 + num2;
  }
}
console.log(MyMath.calculateSum(1, 2)); // Outputs 3
```

Create a namespace called Shape that contains an interface called IShape with a single property called area. Create a class called Rectangle that implements the IShapeinterface and has a method called calculateArea that calculates and returns the area of the rectangle. Test the Rectangle class by creating an instance of it and calling the calculateArea method.

```typescript
namespace Shape {
  export interface IShape {
    area: number;
  }
  export class Rectangle implements IShape {
    constructor(public width: number, public height: number) {}
    calculateArea() {
      this.area = this.width * this.height;
      return this.area;
    }
  }
}
const rectangle = new Shape.Rectangle(10, 20);
console.log(rectangle.calculateArea()); // Outputs 200
```

Create a namespace called MyUtils that contains a class called DateUtils with a static method called getCurrentDate that returns the current date. Create another namespace called MyApp that uses the MyUtils namespace and calls the getCurrentDate method to log the current date to the console.

```typescript
namespace MyUtils {
  export class DateUtils {
    static getCurrentDate() {
      return new Date();
    }
  }
```

```
}
```

```
}
```

```
namespace MyApp {
```

```
console.log(MyUtils.DateUtils.getCurrentDate()); // Outputs current date
```

```
}
```

Create a namespace called Animal **that contains an interface called** IAnimal **with a single property called** name. **Create a second namespace called** Dog **that extends the** Animal **namespace and contains a class called** Dog **that implements the** IAnimalinterface. **Create an instance of the** Dog **class and log its** name **property to the console.**

```
namespace Animal {
```

```
export interface IAnimal {
```

```
name: string;
```

```
}
```

```
}
```

```
namespace Dog {
```

```
import Animal = Animal;
```

```
export class Dog implements Animal.IAnimal {
```

```
constructor(public name: string) {}
```

```
}
```

```
}
```

```
const dog = new Dog.Dog("Buddy");
```

```
console.log(dog.name); // Outputs "Buddy"
```

Create a namespace called MyMath **that contains a function called** calculateSum **that takes two numbers as arguments and returns their sum. Create a second namespace called** MyApp **that also contains a function called** calculateSum **that takes three numbers as arguments and returns their sum. Use the** namespace merging **feature to merge the** MyMath **namespace into the** MyApp **namespace and test the** calculateSum **function by calling it and logging the result to the console.**

```
namespace MyMath {
```

```
export function calculateSum(num1: number, num2: number) {
```

```
return num1 + num2;
```

```
}
```

```
}
```

```
namespace MyApp {
```

```
export function calculateSum(num1: number, num2: number, num3: number) {
```

```
return num1 + num2 + num3;
```

```
}
```

```
MyMath.calculateSum = calculateSum;

console.log(MyMath.calculateSum(1, 2, 3)); // Outputs 6

}
```

MODULES IN TYPESCRIPT

Modules are an essential part of any large-scale application in Typescript. They allow you to organize your code into reusable units that can be imported and used in other parts of your application. In this article, we will cover the basics of modules in Typescript, including how to declare and import them, as well as how to use them to organize and structure your code.

What are Modules in Typescript?

Modules in Typescript are used to organize and structure your code into reusable units. They can contain functions, classes, interfaces, and even other modules, and can be imported and used in other parts of your application. Modules are a powerful tool for separating concerns and ensuring that your code is easy to understand and maintain.

Declaring Modules

There are two ways to declare a module in Typescript: using the export keyword and using the namespacekeyword.

To declare a module using the export keyword, you simply need to add the export keyword in front of any functions, classes, or interfaces that you want to make available for use in other parts of your application. For example:

```typescript
export function sayHello(name: string) {
  console.log(`Hello, ${name}!`);
}
export class User {
  constructor(public name: string, public age: number) {}
}
```

To declare a module using the namespace keyword, you can use the following syntax:

```typescript
namespace MyModule {
  export function sayHello(name: string) {
    console.log(`Hello, ${name}!`);
  }
  export class User {
    constructor(public name: string, public age: number) {}
  }
}
```

```
}
```

Importing Modules

To import a module in Typescript, you can use the import keyword and specify the name of the module and the functions, classes, or interfaces that you want to import. For example:

```
import { sayHello } from "./myModule";
import { User } from "./myModule";
sayHello("John"); // Outputs "Hello, John!"
const user = new User("John", 30);
```

You can also use the import * as syntax to import all the exports of a module into a single object:

```
import * as myModule from "./myModule";
myModule.sayHello("John"); // Outputs "Hello, John!"
const user = new myModule.User("John", 30);
```

Exporting and Importing Types

In addition to exporting and importing functions and classes, you can also export and import types in Typescript. To do this, you can use the export type syntax:

```
export type User = {
  name: string;
  age: number;
};
```

To import a type, you can use the import type syntax:

```
import type { User } from "./myModule";
const user: User = {
  name: "John",
  age: 30,
};
```

Using Modules to Organize Code

One of the main benefits of using modules in Typescript is that they allow you to organize and structure your code in a logical and easy-to-understand way. For example, you can use modules to separate different parts of your application into different files and folders, making it easier to find and maintain your code.

You can also use modules to organize your code by feature or functionality. For example, you might have a separate module for handling user authentication, a separate module for managing data storage, and a separate module for handling UI components. This makes it easier to understand and maintain your code, as well as to reuse code between different parts of your application.

Conclusion

Modules are an essential part of any large-scale Typescript application, and are a powerful tool for organizing and structuring your code. They allow you to declare and import functions, classes, interfaces, and even other modules, and are a great way to ensure that your code is easy to understand and maintain.

Exercises

To review these concepts, we will go through a series of exercises designed to test your understanding and apply what you have learned.

Create a module called MathUtils **that contains a function called** add **that takes in two numbers and returns their sum. Import and use the** add **function in another file.**

Create a module called User **that contains a class with the same name. The class should have three properties:** name, age, **and** email. **Add an** introduce **method to the class that outputs the user's name and email. Import and use the** User **class in another file.**

Create a module called Product **that contains an interface with the same name. The interface should have two properties:** name **and** price. **Create a function called** calculateTotalPrice **that takes in an array of** Product **interfaces and returns the total price of all the products. Import and use the** Product **interface and the** calculateTotalPrice **function in another file.**

Create a module called Utils **that exports multiple functions:** add, subtract, multiply, **and** divide. **Each function should take in two numbers and return the result of the corresponding mathematical operation. Import and use these functions in another file.**

Create a module called Color **that exports an enum with the same name. The enum should contain the colors red, green, and blue. Create a function called** getColorName**that takes in a color value and returns the corresponding color name. Import and use the** Color **enum and the** getColorName **function in another file.**

Solutions

Create a module called MathUtils **that contains a function called** add **that takes in two numbers and returns their sum. Import and use the** add **function in another file.**
MathUtils.ts

```
export function add(a: number, b: number) {
  return a + b;
}
```

main.ts

```
import { add } from "./MathUtils";
console.log(add(2, 3)); // Outputs 5
```

Create a module called User **that contains a class with the same name. The class should have three properties:** name, age, **and** email. **Add an** introduce **method to the class that outputs the user's name and email. Import and use the** User **class in another file.**

User.ts

```
export class User {
constructor(public name: string, public age: number, public email: string) {}
introduce() {
  console.log(`Hi, my name is ${this.name} and my email is ${this.email}.`);
}
}
```

main.ts

```
import { User } from "./User";
const user = new User("John", 30, "john@example.com");
user.introduce(); // Outputs "Hi, my name is John and my email is john@example.com."
```

Create a module called Product **that contains an interface with the same name. The interface should have two properties:** name **and** price. **Create a function called** calculateTotalPrice **that takes in an array of** Product **interfaces and returns the total price of all the products. Import and use the** Product **interface and the** calculateTotalPrice **function in another file.**
Product.ts

```
export interface Product {
 name: string;
 price: number;
}
export function calculateTotalPrice(products: Product[]) {
 return products.reduce((total, product) => total + product.price, 0);
}
```

main.ts

```
import { Product, calculateTotalPrice } from "./Product";
const products: Product[] = [
 { name: "Product 1", price: 10 },
 { name: "Product 2", price: 20 },
 { name: "Product 3", price: 30 },
];
console.log(calculateTotalPrice(products)); // Outputs 60
```

Create a module called Utils **that exports multiple functions:** add, subtract, multiply, **and** divide. **Each function should take in two numbers and return the result of the corresponding mathematical operation. Import and use these functions in another file.**
Utils.ts

```typescript
export function add(a: number, b: number) {
  return a + b;
}
export function subtract(a: number, b: number) {
  return a - b;
}
export function multiply(a: number, b: number) {
  return a * b;
}
export function divide(a: number, b: number) {
  return a / b;
}
```

main.ts

```typescript
import { add, subtract, multiply, divide } from "./Utils";
console.log(add(2, 3)); // Outputs 5
console.log(subtract(2, 3)); // Outputs -1
console.log(multiply(2, 3)); // Outputs 6
console.log(divide(2, 3)); // Outputs 0.6666666666666666
```

Create a module called Color **that exports an enum with the same name. The enum should contain the colors red, green, and blue. Create a function called** getColorName**that takes in a color value and returns the corresponding color name. Import and use the** Color **enum and the** getColorName **function in another file.**
Color.ts

```typescript
export enum Color {
  Red,
  Green,
  Blue,
}
export function getColorName(color: Color) {
  switch (color) {
    case Color.Red:
      return "Red";
    case Color.Green:
      return "Green";
    case Color.Blue:
```

```
    return "Blue";
  }
}
```

main.ts

```
import { Color, getColorName } from "./Color";
console.log(getColorName(Color.Red)); // Outputs "Red"
console.log(getColorName(Color.Green)); // Outputs "Green"
console.log(getColorName(Color.Blue)); // Outputs "Blue"
```

INTEGRATING TYPESCRIPT WITH POPULAR JAVASCRIPT LIBRARIES AND FRAMEWORKS (E.G. REACT, ANGULAR)

Typescript is a popular static type checking language that can be used with many JavaScript libraries and frameworks to provide an extra layer of type safety and organization to your code. In this article, we will explore how to integrate Typescript with two popular libraries: React and Angular.

Integrating Typescript with Angular

One of the most popular JavaScript frameworks for building web applications is Angular. Angular is built with Typescript and it is very easy to integrate Typescript with your Angular projects. In fact, when you create a new Angular project using the Angular CLI, it comes with Typescript support by default.

To start using Typescript with an existing Angular project, you need to install the Typescript compiler. You can do this by running the following command:

```
npm install -g typescript
```

Next, you need to create a tsconfig.json file in the root directory of your project. This file is used to configure the Typescript compiler and tells it how to transpile your Typescript code into JavaScript. You can create a basic tsconfig.json file by running the following command:

```
tsc --init
```

Once you have your tsconfig.json file set up, you can start using Typescript in your Angular project by renaming your .js files to .ts and adding types to your variables and functions.

For example, instead of this:

```
function add(a, b) {
  return a + b;
}
```

You can write this:

```
function add(a: number, b: number): number {
```

```
return a + b;
}
```

By adding types to your variables and functions, you can catch type errors at compile time instead of runtime. This can save you a lot of time debugging and makes your code easier to maintain.

Integrating Typescript with React

React is another popular JavaScript library for building user interfaces. It is not built with Typescript, but it is very easy to integrate Typescript with your React projects.

To start using Typescript with a React project, you need to install the necessary dependencies. You can do this by running the following command:

```
npm install -D @babel/preset-typescript @types/react @types/react-dom
```

Next, you need to create a tsconfig.json file in the root directory of your project. This file is used to configure the Typescript compiler and tells it how to transpile your Typescript code into JavaScript. You can create a basic tsconfig.json file by running the following command:

```
tsc --init
```

Once you have your tsconfig.json file set up, you can start using Typescript in your React project by renaming your .js files to .ts and adding types to your variables and functions.

For example, instead of this:

```
function Hello({ name }) {
  return <div>Hello, {name}</div>;
}
```

You can write this:

```
function Hello({ name }: { name: string }): JSX.Element {
  return <div>Hello, {name}</div>;
}
```

By adding types to your variables and functions, you can catch type errors at compile time instead of runtime. This can save you a lot of time debugging and makes your code easier to maintain.

Conclusion

In conclusion, Typescript is a powerful tool that can help you write safer and more maintainable code, especially when working with large projects or teams. Whether you are using it with React, Angular, or any other JavaScript library or framework, integrating Typescript into your workflow can provide many benefits and make your development experience more enjoyable.

Exercises

To review these concepts, we will go through a series of exercises designed to test your understanding and apply what you have learned.

Create a new Angular project using the Angular CLI and integrate it with Typescript.
Create a new React project using the create-react-app tool and integrate it with Typescript.
Create a new Vue.js project and integrate it with Typescript.
Create a new Ember.js project and integrate it with Typescript.
Create a new AngularJS (1.x) project and integrate it with Typescript.

Solutions

Create a new Angular project using the Angular CLI and integrate it with Typescript.
To create a new Angular project with Typescript, you can use the Angular CLI by running the following command:

```
ng new my-project --style=scss --routing
```

This will create a new Angular project called "my-project" with SCSS style files and routing enabled.

To integrate Typescript with your Angular project, you can use the "–strict" flag:

```
ng new my-project --style=scss --routing --strict
```

Create a new React project using the create-react-app tool and integrate it with Typescript.
To create a new React project with Typescript, you can use the create-react-app tool by running the following command:

```
npx create-react-app my-project --template=typescript
```

This will create a new React project called "my-project" with Typescript enabled and all the necessary configuration files in place.

Create a new Vue.js project and integrate it with Typescript.
To create a new Vue.js project with Typescript, you can use the Vue CLI by running the following command:

```
vue create my-project
```

This will create a new Vue.js project called "my-project" and prompt you to choose additional features. To enable Typescript, you can select the "TypeScript" option.

Create a new Ember.js project and integrate it with Typescript.
To create a new Ember.js project with Typescript, you can use the Ember CLI by running the following command:

```
ember new my-project --yarn --typescript
```

This will create a new Ember.js project called "my-project" with Typescript enabled and all the necessary configuration files in place.

Create a new AngularJS (1.x) project and integrate it with Typescript.

To create a new AngularJS (1.x) project with Typescript, you can use the AngularJS Seed project by running the following command:

```
git clone https://github.com/angular/angular-seed.git my-project
```
```
cd my-project
```
```
npm install
```

This will create a new AngularJS (1.x) project called "my-project" with Typescript enabled and all the necessary configuration files in place. You will also need to install the required dependencies by running the "npm install" command.

BEST PRACTICES FOR USING TYPESCRIPT IN A PROJECT

Typescript is a powerful programming language that provides strong typing, object-oriented concepts, and other features that make it an excellent choice for building large-scale applications. In this article, we'll cover some best practices for using Typescript in a project to ensure that your code is maintainable, scalable, and easy to work with.

Always Use the Latest Version of Typescript

One of the key benefits of using Typescript is that it is constantly being improved and updated. By using the latest version of the language, you'll have access to the newest features and bug fixes, which can help improve the overall quality of your code. To ensure that you're always using the latest version of Typescript, make sure to regularly check for updates and upgrade whenever a new version is released.

Use the "strict" Flag

The "strict" flag is a compiler option that enables a number of additional checks and warnings that can help catch potential problems in your code. For example, it will warn you if you try to use an undeclared variable or if you attempt to assign a value to a read-only property. Enabling the "strict" flag can help you catch errors earlier in the development process and make it easier to maintain your code over time.

Use Type Annotations and Interfaces

Typescript's type system is one of its most powerful features, and using type annotations and interfaces can help you write more reliable and maintainable code. By annotating the types of your variables and function parameters, you can catch mistakes earlier and prevent runtime errors. Interfaces, on the other hand, allow you to define a set of related properties and methods that can be shared across multiple classes.

Leverage the Power of Classes

Typescript's support for classes makes it easy to define complex object-oriented models and abstractions. By using classes, you can define reusable code that can be extended and customized for different purposes. Additionally, classes allow you to use inheritance and polymorphism to create flexible and extensible code bases.

Use Generics Wisely

Generics are a powerful tool in Typescript that allow you to write code that is flexible and reusable.

However, they can also be misused or overused, which can lead to confusing and hard-to-maintain code. To get the most value from generics, make sure to use them in a way that makes sense for your project and to clearly document their usage.

Conclusion

By following these best practices, you can write better Typescript code that is more reliable, maintainable, and scalable. Whether you're new to the language or an experienced developer, taking the time to learn and follow these guidelines will pay off in the long run and make your projects more successful.

Exercises

To review these concepts, we will go through a series of exercises designed to test your understanding and apply what you have learned.

What is the recommended file naming convention for Typescript files?
How can you ensure that your Typescript code adheres to a specific coding style?
How can you improve the performance of your Typescript code?
How can you improve the readability of your Typescript code?
What is the best way to organize your Typescript code in a large project?

Solutions

What is the recommended file naming convention for Typescript files?
It is recommended to use the .ts file extension for Typescript files.

How can you ensure that your Typescript code adheres to a specific coding style?
You can use a linter, such as TSLint, to enforce a specific coding style in your Typescript code.

How can you improve the performance of your Typescript code?
You can use the --noEmitOnError flag in the tsc compiler to improve the performance of your Typescript code. This flag tells the compiler to skip the emit phase if there are any type checking errors.

How can you improve the readability of your Typescript code?
You can use descriptive names for variables and functions, and add comments to explain the purpose of your code. You can also use interfaces and types to clearly define the shape of your data.

What is the best way to organize your Typescript code in a large project?
It is recommended to use modules and namespaces to organize your code into logical units. You can also use external modules, which are compiled into separate files, to further break down your code into manageable chunks.

TIPS AND TRICKS FOR DEBUGGING TYPESCRIPT CODE

Debugging Typescript code can be a bit trickier than debugging regular JavaScript code, since the compiled code may not always match the original Typescript code. However, there are a few tools and techniques that can make debugging Typescript code easier.

Using the Typescript Compiler Flags

One way to make debugging Typescript code easier is by using the appropriate compiler flags. The --sourceMap flag generates source maps, which allow you to debug the original Typescript code rather than the compiled JavaScript code. The --inlineSourceMap flag includes the source map as a data URL in the compiled JavaScript file, which can be useful for debugging in certain environments.

The --inlineSources flag includes the original Typescript source code in the source map, which can be useful for debugging when the source maps are not available. However, this can increase the size of the compiled JavaScript file, so it should be used sparingly.

Using a Debugger

Most modern code editors and IDEs have built-in debuggers that can be used to debug Typescript code. These debuggers typically allow you to set breakpoints, step through code, and inspect variables.

To use a debugger, you will need to configure the debugger to use the source maps generated by the Typescript compiler. This typically involves specifying the location of the source maps and the root directory of the Typescript files.

Console Logging

Sometimes, using a debugger is not practical or possible, and in these cases, console logging can be a useful tool for debugging Typescript code. By inserting console.log statements into your code, you can print out the values of variables and expressions to the console, which can help you identify problems in your code.

Tips and Tricks

- Use type assertions to temporarily override the type of a variable. This can be useful for debugging when you suspect that the wrong type is being inferred.
- Use the --strict flag to enable additional type checking and catch more bugs at compile time.

- Use the --noEmitOnError flag to prevent the compiler from generating JavaScript code if there are type errors. This can be useful for catching type errors early on.

If you're having a particularly difficult time debugging your code, you might consider using a debugger. Many code editors have built-in debuggers, or you can use a standalone debugger like the Chrome DevTools. Debuggers allow you to step through your code line by line, see the values of variables at different points in time, and even set breakpoints to pause the execution of your code.

Conclusion

Finally, don't be afraid to ask for help. Whether it's from coworkers, online communities like Stack Overflow, or a mentor, getting a fresh perspective on your code can often lead to a breakthrough in understanding what's going wrong.

Exercises

To review these concepts, we will go through a series of exercises designed to test your understanding and apply what you have learned.

Consider the following code:

```typescript
function add(a: number, b: number): number {
  return a + b;
}
console.log(add(1, '2'));
```

What will be logged to the console?
Consider the following code:

```typescript
interface Point {
  x: number;
  y: number;
}
function printPoint(point: Point): void {
  console.log(`(${point.x}, ${point.y})`);
}
const point = { x: 1, y: 2, z: 3 };
printPoint(point);
```

What will be logged to the console?
Consider the following code:

```typescript
function add(a: number, b: number): number {
  return a + b;
}
console.log(add(1, 2));
```

How could you use a debugger to understand what's happening in this code?
How can you use the Typescript compiler to catch type errors during development?
What is the "debugger" keyword and how can it be used in Typescript?

Solutions

What will be logged to the console?
An error will be thrown because the add function expects two numbers, but a string is being passed as the second argument.

What will be logged to the console?
The point (1, 2) will be logged to the console because the printPoint function only expects the x and y properties of the Point interface, and those are the only properties provided in the point object.

How could you use a debugger to understand what's happening in this code?
You could set a breakpoint on the first line of the add function. Then, when you run the code in the debugger, it will pause execution at that point. You can then step through the code line by line to see how the values of a and b are being used to calculate the sum.

How can you use the Typescript compiler to catch type errors during development?
The Typescript compiler can catch type errors during development by using the "strict" option in the "tsconfig.json" file. When this option is set to "true", the compiler will perform additional type checking and will report any type errors it finds. This can be very helpful for catching issues early on and ensuring that your code is correct before it is compiled and run. To enable the "strict" option, you can include the following in your "tsconfig.json" file:

```
{
"compilerOptions": {
  "strict": true
 }
}
```

What is the "debugger" keyword and how can it be used in Typescript?
The "debugger" keyword is a way to pause the execution of your code at a certain point, allowing you to inspect variables and step through the code line by line. To use it in Typescript, you can simply include the "debugger" keyword in your code where you want to pause the execution. For example:

```
function myFunction() {
let x = 1;
let y = 2;
debugger; // execution will pause here, allowing you to inspect x and y
let z = x + y;

}
```

THANK YOU

Thank you again for choosing "Learn TypeScript I hope it helps you in your journey to learn TypeScript and achieve your goals. Please take a small portion of your time and share this with your friends and family and write a review for this book. I hope your programming journey does not end here. If you are interested, check out other books that I have or find more coding challenges at: https://codeofcode.org